In this book, David Rowland traces the history of piano pedalling from its beginning in the eighteenth century to its first maturity in the middle of the nineteenth century and beyond. Pedalling technique became a major feature of nineteenth-century piano performance at a time of new developments in piano construction and many composers were inspired to write innovative works for the literature. Rowland examines this through the technique and music of composer-pianists such as Beethoven, Liszt and Chopin. In addition, he follows the transition from harpsichord and clavichord to piano in the music of Mozart and his contemporaries and outlines the physical properties of the various stops, levers and pedals available at the different stages of the instrument's development. The book also includes an appendix of translated extracts from three well-known piano tutors.

The book will be of interest to students and scholars of music history and performance practice, as well as to pianists.

CAMBRIDGE MUSICAL TEXTS AND MONOGRAPHS

General Editors: Howard Mayer Brown, Peter le Huray, John Stevens

A History of Pianoforte Pedalling

CAMBRIDGE MUSICAL TEXTS AND MONOGRAPHS

A History
of Pianoforte Pedalling

DAVID ROWLAND

Lecturer in Music,
The Open University

CAMBRIDGE
UNIVERSITY PRESS

Published by the Press Syndicate of the University of Cambridge
The Pitt Building, Trumpington Street, Cambridge CB2 1RP
40 West 20th Street, New York, NY 10011–4211, USA
10 Stamford Road, Oakleigh, Melbourne 3166, Australia

First published in 1993
Reprinted 1995

Printed in Great Britain at the University Press, Cambridge

A catalogue record for this book is available from the British Library

Library of Congress cataloguing in publication data

Rowland, David.
A history of pianoforte pedalling / David Rowland.
     p.   cm. – (Cambridge musical texts and monographs)
Includes bibliographical references and index.
ISBN 0 521 40266 2
1. Piano – Pedalling – History. 2. Piano – Performance – History.
I. Title. II. Series.
MT227.R72 1993
786.2′ 1938′ 09 dc20 92–37065 CIP

ISBN 0521 40266 2 hardback

SN

Contents

viii   Contents

Acknowledgements

This book is the result of many years' research and I would like to thank several people whose help has been invaluable at various stages. First of all, my thanks are due to Glyn Jenkins, whose work on the performance of early piano music inspired this project. I am also grateful to him for supplying the translation of Milchmeyer's chapter on pedalling for the Appendix. Howard Ferguson and Virginia Pleasants helped to see the project through its early stages and Julian Rushton provided invaluable assistance and support as it took shape. More recently I have been greateful to Richard Maunder, Peter le Huray and Penny Souster for their help and advice.

A work of this nature would not have been possible without a great deal of assistance from a number of libraries and their staff. In particular I would like to mention Margaret Cranmer of the Rowe Library, King's College, Cambridge, Hugh Taylor, Richard Andrewes, the staff of the University Library, Cambridge, and the staff of the Pendlebury Library, Cambridge. I would also like to thank the staff of the British Library, London, and the Bibliothèque Nationale, Paris for their help.

Finally, I would like to thank my wife, Ruth, and children, Kate, Hannah and Eleanor, without whose support and patience this book would not have come into being.

Abbreviations

AMZ	*Allgemeine musikalische Zeitung*
EM	*Early Music*
GSJ	*Galpin Society Journal*
JAMIS	*Journal of the American Musical Instrument Society*
JAMS	*Journal of the American Musicological Society*
ML	*Music and Letters*
MQ	*Musical Quarterly*
MT	*Musical Times*

Introduction

The importance of the pedal as an adjunct to artistic piano playing can hardly be overestimated. It is not too much to say that the effect of almost all modern music (from the earliest compositions of Thalberg and Liszt) depends upon its skillful use, and yet no question of technic has been so much neglected. While touch has been analyzed in the most minute manner, every movement of finger, wrist and arm noted with the greatest accuracy, the study of the pedal, as Herr Schmitt remarks, has hardly gone beyond the standpoint of instinctive feeling on the part of the player.

This was Frederick Law's assessment in 1893, given in the introduction to his translation of Hans Schmitt's *Das Pedal des Claviers* (Vienna 1875). His remarks are entirely justified. Apart from some chapters of a rather general nature in nineteenth-century piano tutors, there had been no detailed study of the subject prior to Schmitt's. Consequently, assessing the precise characteristics of the pedalling techniques of major nineteenth-century figures such as Liszt or Thalberg is far from easy, and it is still more difficult to discover the way in which the earliest pianists such as Mozart may, or may not, have used the devices which were common on pianos of their day.

Since the appearance of Schmitt's book towards the end of the nineteenth century a number of pedalling tutors have been published which explore the details of the instrument's mechanism as well as technique. More recently there has been a growing awareness of some historical aspects of the subject. One of the best modern studies which draws all of these strands together is Joseph Banowetz's book *The Pianist's Guide to Pedalling*. There is, however, a fundamental weakness in most of the historical studies which have been published: they tend to concentrate on a single composer, or small group of composers, rather than reviewing broader trends. A number of authors, for example, have written on Beethoven's pedalling – undoubtedly a crucial subject for any pianist – without fully understanding his personal idiosyncrasies. Beethoven's use of the una corda, for example, can only be understood properly in the context of the performing styles of his contemporaries. Conversely, some apparent peculiarities of his pedalling, such as his directions to depress

I

the sustaining pedal for passages lasting several bars, turn out to be quite unexceptional in the light of similar passages in works by other composers.

The purpose of this volume is to trace the history of pianoforte pedalling from its beginnings in the eighteenth century to its first maturity in the middle of the nineteenth and early twentieth centuries. In this way, the major composers for the instrument are set into the context of the different schools of pianoforte playing which have existed during various phases of the instrument's history.[1] These schools were widely recognised in their day. Pianists in late eighteenth-century London, for example, played in a very different style from their Viennese contemporaries, and the 'Paris style' of the 1830s and 1840s raised many conservative eyebrows, especially in Germany. Schools were distinguished by various emphases in technique; but their differences were perhaps nowhere more obvious than in the pedalling styles which their members adopted.

A variety of questions needs to be considered in a history of pedalling. A fundamental issue concerning the music of eighteenth- and nineteenth-century composers is the type of instrument for which composers were writing – an issue which strangely receives little attention in histories of the piano. Figures such as Mozart and Clementi played not only pianos, but harpsichords and clavichords as well. Before even considering whether a passage in their music might be pedalled it is therefore necessary to know for which type of keyboard instrument a work was written. For this reason the whole of Chapter 1 is devoted to the transition from the older keyboard instruments to the piano. If investigation of these issues establishes that a work was written for the piano, it is then necessary to have some knowledge of the bewildering array of stops, levers and pedals that appeared on instruments at various phases of the piano's history. Chapter 2 summarises this information in such a way as to make it easily available for quick reference.

If it is known what type of piano a composer was writing for, it cannot necessarily be assumed that he intended all, or indeed any, of the tone-modifying devices to be used. This issue becomes more difficult the further back one goes in the piano's history. Pedal markings did not occur in piano music until the 1790s – after Mozart's death – so the historian has to draw on information in tutors, descriptions of performances, and any scrap of evidence to trace the development of pedalling for most of the eighteenth century. Because the evidence is so varied, and yet so scarce, and because this is the first crucial phase of the history of pedalling, the whole of Part II is taken up with the techniques of the early pianists. Chapter 3 is devoted to comments made in a wide variety of eighteenth and early nineteenth-century literature. Chapter 4 examines the earliest discussions of pedalling in keyboard tutors, and Chapter 5 reviews the first pedal markings in the music itself.

The beginning of the nineteenth century saw a proliferation of printed sources of all kinds, yet it remains surprisingly difficult to pinpoint detailed developments of technique. When, for example, was syncopated pedalling first used and by whom? How much did pianists use the una corda and other pedals which were so common on pianos before the middle of the nineteenth century? How enthusiastic were pianists about the introduction of the third pedal found in the middle on most modern grands? Part III investigates these and related issues.

Pianoforte pedalling is a complex subject, and an important one: the decisions which a pianist makes in this area can change the whole nature of a performance. The conclusions reached by this study will need to be considered by pianists who perform on early instruments as well as those who prefer their modern counterparts. Whilst no attempt is made to suggest how early pedalling might be realised on the modern piano – the extent to which any pianist wishes to do this will inevitably vary – all pianists will need to consider the issues which this book raises if they wish seriously to get to grips with the music they play.

PART I

The instruments

I

The transition from the harpsichord and clavichord to the piano

The early history of the piano

The history of the piano begins in Italy. Bartolomeo Cristofori, the piano's inventor, appears to have begun work on the instrument as early as 1698.[1] His pianos were described in detail by Maffei in 1711:[2] three of them survive in various parts of the world today.[3] Cristofori's work became well known during his lifetime: pianos by him or his pupils were found in Italy and the Iberian Peninsula[4] and a translation of Maffei's description was published in Hamburg by Mattheson in his *Critica Musica* of 1725. In the same year the Augsburg instrument maker Johann Cristoph Leo advertised 'Cimbalen ohne Kiele' ('harpsichords without quills') – presumably pianos – in the Viennese press.[5] Meanwhile, Schröter had exhibited some experimental instruments in Dresden.[6]

By 1758 the piano was apparently known in a number of places, according to Adlung in his *Anleitung zu der musikalischen Gelahrheit* (Erfurt, p. 563). He had not seen one himself, but he does nevertheless mention one of the most important early makers of the instrument in Germany, Friederici. Adlung returned to the history of the piano in a later publication in which he goes into far greater detail, devoting much space to the work of another maker, Gottfried Silbermann.[7] Silbermann was making pianos in the early 1730s, but his most famous instruments were those purchased by Frederick the Great in the 1740s, two of which still survive, along with another instrument, now in Nuremberg.[8] The Silbermann family were probaby the most important makers of the piano in the mid eighteenth century. Gottfried's work was continued by his pupil and nephew Johann Heinrich, who worked in Strasbourg, and whose pianos were probably the first to appear in France. A number of references to pianos by members of the Silbermann family are to be found in the mid-eighteenth-century literature, underlining their significance.

From Germany, the piano spread both to England and to France. In 1755 an English cleric, William Mason, bought a piano in Hamburg.[9] Shortly afterwards a number of German instrument makers arrived in London. In 1763 one of them, Frederic Neubauer, advertised the sale of 'harpsichords, pianofortes, lyrachords and claffichords'.[10] Whether these instruments were imported or made locally is not clear; neither do we know whether any were sold. But within three years another German émigré, Johannes Zumpe, was making the square pianos that were to become so popular in the decade that followed.[11]

In France, a piano was advertised in the press in 1759.[12] It is not clear who placed the advertisement, but it may have had something to do with the arrival in Paris during the previous year of Johann Eckard and Johann Andreas Stein, who visited the workshop of Johann Heinrich Silbermann *en route*. The purpose of that visit remains uncertain, but whatever happened, Silbermann was certainly hoping to make an impact on the French market in 1761, when his pianos were named in a newspaper advertisement.[13]

Keyboard players to c.1760

By the 1760s the piano was known in many, if not most, major European cities. This is not to say, however, that all prominent keyboard players can be assumed to have preferred the piano to other keyboard instruments by that date. Whilst it is certainly true that some performers, such as Scarlatti and Bach, had experience of the new instrument at an early stage, they were not necessarily won over to it completely. Indeed, the harpsichord and clavichord lived on in performance alongside the piano well into the last quarter of the century.

Domenico Scarlatti spent several months in Florence, where Cristofori worked, in 1702. In 1719 he became attached to the court in Lisbon, where he taught Maria Barbara, later Queen of Spain. In 1732 the earliest known music specifically for the piano was published in Florence, but the dedicatee of these sonatas was Don Antonio of Portugal, patron and pupil of Scarlatti.[14] Meanwhile, Scarlatti had moved to Spain with Maria Barbara. Here he stayed until his death in 1757. The following year an inventory was made of Maria Barbara's instruments which included five pianos made in Florence.[15] In addition to these instruments, Scarlatti may well have played one owned by his colleague Farinelli. It was an instrument by Ferrini, one of Cristofori's pupils, to which Farinelli became very attached, as Burney noted when the two met in 1770.[16]

As Scarlatti was so closely associated with pianos it is tempting to assume that his sonatas were written for them; but the evidence suggests otherwise. Of the five pianos known from the 1758 inventory to have belonged to Maria Barbara, two had previously been converted into harpsichords – a strange occurrence since their intricate piano action must have been very costly. Presumably Maria Barbara, or Scarlatti himself, had expressed dissatisfaction with the pianos (as did a number of eighteenth-century musicians). Of the three remaining pianos in the inventory, two had a range of four and a half octaves while the third was smaller still, with a range of a little over four octaves. In contrast, three of the harpsichords mentioned in the inventory had a full five-octave compass. The greater range of these instruments perhaps suggests that they were used as solo instruments (many of Scarlatti's sonatas use a five-octave keyboard), the smaller pianos being better suited to continuo or accompanying roles. On the other hand, there are also many Scarlatti sonatas whose tessitura would have fitted the pianos, and until further information comes to light it is impossible to say exactly how often and for which works the pianos might have been used.

J. S. Bach's association with the piano is partly documented by Johann Friedrich Agricola, court composer in Berlin, himself a keen student and advocate of the new instrument.[17] He relates how Bach tried out one of Silbermann's pianos and expressed some dissatisfaction with it. Bach approved later instruments by the same maker, however, and it was one of these that he played on a visit to Frederick the Great's court in 1747. A contemporary newspaper relates how the king

went at Bach's entrance to the so-called forte and piano, condescending also to play, in person and without any preparation, a theme to be executed by Capellmeister Bach in a fugue. This was done so happily by the aforementioned Capellmeister that not only His Majesty was pleased to show his satisfaction thereat, but also all those present were seized with astonishment.[18]

It was this visit to Berlin that gave rise to the *Musical Offering* on the theme played by the king, and it has been suggested that Bach's improvisation formed the basis of the three-part ricercar from that work.[19] Two years later Bach seems to have been acting as Silbermann's agent: a voucher for the sale of one of his pianos to Count Branitzky of Poland was signed by Bach and dated 9 May 1749.[20] Presumably Bach was confident enough in these instruments to give them his endorsement, though whether he had access to one on which he played regularly himself is not known.

The evidence for the use of the piano rather than the harpsichord or clavichord in the first half of the eighteenth century is far from conclusive. There were certainly pianos in parts of southern Europe and Germany and these instruments were known to some of the leading keyboard players of the time, such as Scarlatti and Bach. It is far from clear, however, whether performers regarded them simply as curiosities, or as serious rivals to other keyboard instruments.

Keyboard players after c.1760

The progress of the piano was much quicker after the middle of the century. We have already seen how it was introduced into France and England in the 1750s. In the decade that followed, its profile was enhanced by its use in public performance all over Europe, and by the publication of music which specifically mentions the instrument. On 17 May 1763 Herr Schmid played what was almost certainly a concerto on a piano in the Vienna Burgtheatre.[21] In 1767 contemporary newspapers advertised a concert on 16 May in which Miss Brickler, a singer, was to be accompanied on a piano by Charles Dibdin in Covent Garden. This was the piano's first recorded public outing in London and it was followed by solo appearances in 1768 (although solo piano music had been published two years earlier in London).[22] In France, the piano appeared for the first time in public in 1768, when Mademoiselle Le Chantre played some solo pieces by Romain de Brasseur at the Concert Spirituel.[23]

What sorts of pianos were used for these public performances? Nothing is known about the instrument used for the first Viennese public performance. As makers in Italy and southern Germany were producing both grand and square pianos, either could have been used on this and other occasions. The situation was different in England, however. By the late 1760s Zumpe had made a good number of square pianos, to judge from the number that still survive as well as references to these instruments in contemporary accounts. In contrast, Backers, the first maker of English grands, probably did not begin making his pianos much before 1770. By the time of his death in 1778 he seems only to have made about sixty grand pianos.[24] The earliest performances on the piano in England were therefore on squares, while grands were presumably used with increasing frequency from around 1770.

French makers seem to have been very slow to produce pianos. Only in 1770 do we know with any certainty that they were being made in Paris,[25] though the presence of one in Blanchet's workshop in 1766 might suggest an earlier date.[26] Before then there was a trickle of imports, especially of Johann Heinrich Silbermann's instruments, as we have seen already. There must surely have been a few pianos in Paris to justify the mention of the instrument in the first editions of Eckard's sonatas opp. 1 and 2 (Paris 1763 and 1764 respectively).

The trend accelerated dramatically in Paris after 1770. Zumpe was there during that year, no doubt furthering his business interests.[27] He was not alone: Burney is known to have helped Diderot in the purchase of a Zumpe square,[28] and J. C. Bach acted as Zumpe's agent in sending Madame Brillon one at about the same time.[29] Clearly the marketing strategy from London was very vigorous, so much so that by 1773 Trouflaut observed that almost all pianos sold in Paris came from London.[30] His comment is borne out by the figures relating to the instruments confiscated from the nobility during the revolution: squares by Zumpe, his successor Schoene, and others such as Beck and Pohlman far outnumber any other sort of piano.[31]

These imports from London were almost always square pianos rather than grands, as were the instruments made in Paris after 1770. It was only in the late 1780s that grands began to appear. Taskin probably started to make them around 1786[32] and at the time of his death in 1793 there were several in various states of completion in his workshop.[33] Another Parisian maker, Goermans, had both grands and squares in his workshop in 1789.[34] But Erard, the foremost of all the French piano makers of the eighteenth century, did not start to make grands until 1797, after his return from England.[35] For most of the 1770s and 1780s, then, it seems that French pianists would have been playing on squares rather than grands.

Were all later eighteenth-century keyboard players in favour of the new instrument? The answer to this question is quite clearly no. Whilst pianos were becoming increasingly available all over Europe as the century progressed, the older harpsichord and clavichord remained common in performance until at least the 1780s. Several factors point to this conclusion. Dr Burney, for example, made extensive and detailed comments on keyboard performance in his accounts of his European tours. His remarks on his journey through Germany and Austria – where so much early activity concerning the piano had taken place – are particularly instructive.

Burney set off in the middle of 1772. As he passed through towns and cities in the north of Europe such as Brussels, Antwerp, Koblenz, Frankfurt and others, he heard only harpsichords. In Ludwigsburg he met Christian Friedrich Daniel Schubart. According to Burney 'he played on the clavichord, with great delicacy and expression' to begin with, and later in the day he played a great deal more on the 'harpsichord, organ, piano forte and clavichord'.[36] Burney then travelled on to Munich, where he heard four different peformers play on the harpsichord, but none on the piano.

Finally, Burney arrived in Vienna. Here he met a number of competent amateurs including the Countess Thun, a friend of the Mozarts, whom he heard play the harpsichord. He also met a good number of important professionals. Wagenseil, for example, played the harpsichord to him on a number of occasions. Gluck played to him on what he described as a 'bad harpsichord' and another composer, Hasse, also played the harpsichord for him. Burney describes Vanhal as a harpsichordist too, but actually heard him play the clavichord. In fact, out of a total of some fifteen accounts of keyboard playing in Vienna (mostly in private houses, but including some public concerts) there is only one relating to the piano; and this was a rather miserable occasion:

I went to Mr L'Augier's concert, which was begun by the child of eight or nine years old, whom he had mentioned to me before, and who played two difficult lessons of Scarlatti, with three or four by Mr Becke, upon a small, and not good Piano forte.[37]

From Vienna Burney went to Dresden and Leipzig, both still suffering from the effects of the Seven Years War. No performances on pianos were recorded in either city.

Further north, as Burney entered the region where makers such as Silbermann and Friederici had been active, he encountered more pianos. In

Berlin, where Frederick the Great had acquired several of Silbermann's pianos in the 1740s, he first called on Agricola, who

received me very politely; and though he was indisposed, and had just been blooded, he obligingly sat down to a fine piano forte, which I was desirous of hearing, and touched it in a truly great style.[38]

Agricola was keenly interested in the piano. It was he who had provided Adlung with historical information on the instrument,[39] and he was also interested in the use to which it had been put in Berlin: he comments that the piano had been used on one occasion, and with good effect, in the Berlin opera.[40] Indeed, it may well be that the piano's role in Berlin was largely an accompanying one: both C. P. E. Bach and Quantz wrote about its use in this way, and when Burney visited the King's music room where he regularly played flute solos and concertos accompanied by a small orchestra it was a Silbermann piano that he noticed there – perhaps the instrument that J. S. Bach had played in 1747.[41] Despite the apparently frequent performances on pianos in Berlin, however, the harpsichord and clavichord were still used. Kirnberger, for example, played both, according to Burney.[42]

The last important centre in Burney's itinerary was Hamburg. One of his first calls here was on C. P. E. Bach, who improvised on a new piano, perhaps the Friederici instrument mentioned in the inventory of Bach's possessions at his death, or an instrument he was selling on to someone else.[43] A little later, Burney was taken to a concert where he heard an accompanied harpsichord sonatina. A few days after that, at Hasse's urging, he was back at C. P. E. Bach's house listening to him play his Silbermann clavichord, an activity for which Bach had become famous.[44] Clearly all three keyboard instruments were regularly in use at the time in Hamburg. Yet the piano had been known there from Mattheson's translation of Maffei's description in 1725.[45] It was also in Hamburg that William Mason purchased his piano in 1755.[46] Even in the later 1770s the piano seems to have been considered only as one of a number of options: on 24 February 1777, for example, one of C. P. E. Bach's pupils played a solo in public on the piano, but in the same programme played a concerto on the harpsichord.[47]

If the situation in Germany and Austria was rather confused in the 1770s, it was scarcely less so elsewhere in Europe. Despite the fact that the piano had begun to appear in Paris in the late 1750s, not everyone was in favour of its use. Daquin had the privilege of playing one of Silbermann's pianos in 1769 but confessed that he found it 'a delicate dish, of which one will soon be sick' compared with the solid 'bread' of the harpsichord.[48] Five years later Voltaire heard Balbastre play some noels on the piano, which he then described as a 'cauldron-maker's instrument'.[49] At the Concert Spirituel, where the piano had first appeared in 1768, the instrument's progress was slow. In

1778, for example, the piano only seems to have been used in a symphonie concertante along with parts for solo violin and harp, whereas the harpsichord was used in a trio and, on another occasion, in a concerto. The following year it was the harpsichord's turn to be used in a symphonie concertante. But later in the same year a concerto was played on the piano, a significant event which may have marked the maturity of the instrument in Paris: more piano concertos were performed in 1780 and in the years that followed.[50]

In England the widespread use of the piano seems to have developed rather earlier, perhaps as a result of the more robust English grands that appeared from the late 1760s. James Hook was probaby the first in London to play a concerto on the instrument in 1768. Others, however, were more cautious. Clementi, for example, the so-called 'father of the pianoforte', played the harpsichord on six out of his seven public appearances between 1775 and 1780. On the one occasion that he used a piano it was for a duet; concertos were played by him on the harpsichord.[51]

All over Europe up to the 1780s the harpsichord, and to an extent the clavichord, were used alongside the piano as alternative instruments. In certain circumstances the harpsichord seems to have been preferred – notably in concertos, according to some of the evidence in Paris and London. The reason for this is probably the superiority of the harpsichord over the early piano in projecting its sound. But on other occasions the piano was better – in accompanying, for example, as in Berlin. Composers such as Clementi and Mozart, therefore, who are conventionally supposed to have written their keyboard music for the piano, would have played many of their earlier works on an older keyboard instrument.[52] It was only in the 1780s that the piano seems finally to have dethroned the harpsichord and clavichord.

2

Stops, levers and pedals

The harpsichord

Because of the way in which keyboard instruments were used interchangeably in the eighteenth century it is not unreasonable to assume that attitudes to stops, levers and pedals on one instrument were transferred to another. Certainly there were national trends in instrument making common to both the harpsichord and the piano: countries, for example, which tended to use knee levers on harpsichords also tended to use them on pianos, and countries where the number of devices used on harpsichords was comparatively large also tended to see extravagant numbers of pedals or levers on pianos. It is therefore appropriate to consider briefly the history of stops, levers and pedals on the harpsichord before pursuing their use on the piano.

Early developments

In 1713 François Couperin observed that 'the harpsichord is perfect as to its range, and brilliant in its own right; but since it is impossible to increase or diminish the sound I shall always be grateful to those who, by infinite art supported by good taste, succeed in making the instrument capable of expression'.[1] Most of the devices that were added to the instrument at various stages of its history were attempts to rectify this defect. As early as 1676 Thomas Mace, Clerk of Trinity College, Cambridge, described an instrument which he called a 'pedal':

the *Pedal*, (an *Instrument* of a *Late Invention*, contriv'd (as I have been inform'd) by one Mr *John Hayward* of *London*, a most *Excellent Kind of Instrument for a Consort*, and far beyond all *Harpsicons* or *Organs*, that I yet ever heard of, (I mean either for *Consort*, or *Single Use*;) . . .

Concerning *This Instrument*, (call'd the *Pedal* because It is contriv'd to give *Varieties* with the *Foot*) I shall bestow a few *Lines* in making mention of, in regard It is not very commonly used, or known; because *Few make of Them Well*, and *Fewer* will go to the *Price of Them: Twenty Pounds* being the *Ordinary Price of One*; but the *Great Patron of Musick in his Time*, Sir *Robert Bolles*, (who, in the *University*, I had the *Happiness to Initiate*, in

14

This High Art) had *Two of Them*, the one I remember at 30 1. and the other at 50 1. very *Admirable Instruments*.

This Instrument is in *Shape and Bulk* just like a *Harpsicon*; only it differs in the *Order* of *It*, Thus, *viz*. There is made right underneath the *Keys*, near the *Ground*, a kind of *Cubbord*, or *Box*, which opens with a little *Pair* of *Doors*, in which *Box* the *Performer* sets both his *Feet*, resting them upon his *Heels*, (his *Toes* a little turning up) touching nothing, till such time as he has a *Pleasure* to employ them; which is after this manner, *viz*. There being right underneath his *Toes 4 little Pummels of Wood*, under *each Foot 2*, any one of *Those* 4 he may *Tread* upon at his *Pleasure*; which by the *Weight of his Foot drives a Spring*, and so *Causeth the whole Instrument to Sound*, either *Soft* or *Loud, according as he shall chuse to Tread any of them down*; (for without the *Foot*, so us'd, *Nothing Speaks*.)

The *out-side* of the *Right Foot* drives *One*, and the *In-side* of the same *Foot* drives other; so that by treading his *Foot* a little awry, either outward or inward, he causeth a *Various Stop* to be heard, *at his Pleasure*; and if he clap down his *Foot Flat*, then he takes *Them both*, at the same time, (which is a 3d, *Variety*, and *Louder*.)

Then has he ready, under his Left *Foot*, 2 other *Various Stops*, and by the like *Order* and *Motion* of the Foot he can immediately give you 3 other *Varieties*, either *Softer* or *Louder*, as with the *Right Foot* before mentioned, he did.

So that thus you may perceive that he has several *Various Stops* at Pleasure; and all *Quick and Nimble*, by the *Ready Turn* of the Foot.

And by *This Pritty Device*, is *This Instrument made Wonderfully Rare, and Excellent*. So that doubtless it *Excels al Harpsicons*, or *Organs* in the World, for *Admirable Sweetness and Humour, either for a Private, or a Consort use*.[2]

Similar attempts were recorded in various parts of Europe in the first part of the eighteenth century,[3] but as isolated examples.

It was only from around the middle of the eighteenth century that significant numbers of harpsichords were made with tone-modifying devices. These varied from country to country not just in the nature of their mechanism but also in the maner in which they were operated.

Later developments

England

In England, one or two pedals were attached to double-manual instruments depending on the wishes of the client. One was the so-called machine pedal. This allowed the performer to change registration from a 'full' sound to a much quieter one without removing the hands from the keyboard.[4] It occurs regularly on harpsichords from the mid 1760s though its precise origins are difficult to trace. Whether it was invented by Kirkman or Shudi (or by someone else) is unknown; but the machine pedal was standard on double-manual harpsichords by these two makers for the rest of the century.

The second pedal to become a regular feature of English harpsichord manufacture was the swell. Sometimes this was rather a crude mechanism which lifted part of the instrument's lid, but a more complex and effective

'Venetian swell' was also used. This comprised a number of shutters placed over the strings and running parallel with them which could be opened and shut by means of the pedal. The Venetian swell was patented by Shudi in 1769, while lid swells of various sorts were used from as early as 1755.[5]

France

Whilst pedals seem to have been the standard means of operating both the machine and Venetian swell devices in England, French makers preferred more visually discreet knee levers for their sound-modifying devices. Weltman's instrument of 1759, which he presented to the Académie des Sciences, had knee levers which operated the stop knobs in such a way that 'one becomes the master in the execution of a piece, during a passage, and even during a cadenza – not only in producing various echos but even in diminishing or augmenting the sound imperceptibly'.[6] Joseph-Antoine Berger of Grenoble used a knee-lever mechanism in 1762 and Virbès of Paris applied two such devices to a harpsichord four years later in an attempt to obtain *forte* and *piano* effects.[7] Later still, in 1768 (according to the Abbé Trouflaut), Taskin used a knee lever to operate a mechanism closely resembling the English machine pedal.[8] In addition, four or five other knee levers were added to instruments by Taskin to control the individual registers of the harpsichord. Soft leather (*peau de buffle*) plectra were also introduced on one register in an attempt to give the performer the option of a more gentle sound.

Whilst French harpsichord makers preferred knee levers they occasionally used pedals instead. De Laine, for example, advertised a pedal mechanism for swelling and diminishing the sound in the *Mercure de France*, August 1769. Erard made a harpsichord with both knee levers and pedals in 1779[9] and in 1783 the *Almanach musicale* advertised more than one harpsichord with pedals. Even Taskin, who otherwise seems to have preferred knee levers, advertised in 1782 a 'Harpsichord by Couchet made as new and extended by P. Taskin, with exquisite paintings and foot mechanism for varying the performance between 10 and 12 ways'.[10] These references could indicate a change in French preferences from knee levers to pedals; but the fact that both Erard and Taskin subsequently made harpsichords with knee levers suggests other-wise. It would appear that the French were happy to adopt both knee levers and pedals, with a decided preference for the former.

Other countries

Elsewhere in Europe pedals and knee levers do not seem to have been so popular on harpsichords, though they did appear from time to time. An instru-ment constructed by Milchmeyer, for example, boasting three manuals and 'two hundred and fifty changes of tone colour', is described in Cramer's *Magazin der Musik* (1783).[11] Milchmeyer's use of knee levers was commended by the author of the article, who pointed out how much more reliable and sensitive they were than foot pedals, and how they had the advantage of being out of sight, yet within the reach of children. In Italy, Prosperi is reported to have produced an early machine mechanism in 1700.[12] Later, in 1775, an anonymous booklet printed in Rome discusses pedals for operating the registers.[13] Further north, in Sweden, Nils Brelin designed a clavicytherium (an upright harpsichord or spinet) in 1741 with eight variations of tone controlled by pedals. In addition to the harpsichords actually made in these countries, imported instruments were also increasingly common. English makers in particular enjoyed great success as exporters in the second half of the century, and several Shudis and Kirkmans (with pedals) were known in various parts of Europe. Nevertheless, makers outside England and France generally avoided pedals and knee levers in the later eighteenth century.

The pianoforte

To c.1760

As few southern European and German pianos survive from this early period only the most general of observations are possible. Most of these early instruments have one or two devices for modifying the sound, devices which are operated by hand stops rather than knee levers or pedals.

The three surviving Cristofori grands (1720, 1722, 1726) all have one such device. This is the una corda, operated by knobs at either end of the keyboard which enable the performer to move the keyboard laterally.[14] These instruments resemble Italian harpsichords in many ways, suggesting that the una corda was originally thought of in the same way as the registers of the harpsichord, enabling the performer to use one or both sets of eight-foot strings. Other southern European makers who imitated Cristofori's design seem to have followed him in the use of a single hand stop for the una corda.[15]

Cristofori's design was modified in Germany. There are two devices on each of the three surviving Gottfried Silbermann grands (1746, 1749, undated). One of these is a rather curious stop whose aim seems to be to make the instrument sound like a harpsichord: pieces of ivory are brought into contact with the strings just at the point where the hammer strikes.[16] The other stop raises the dampers from the strings, serving the same purpose as the right pedal on modern pianos. This device was probably added in imitation of the dulcimer, an instrument which had been made popular in Germany and elsewhere by Hebenstreit, the most famous 'panalonist' of the century (Silbermann had made seveal large dulcimers for Hebenstreit – see Chapter 3).[17] The combination of the sustaining stop and some other hand-operated device (usually for diminishing the sound) was used on pianos by other makers such as Friederici[18] and was to become the most popular disposition of the eighteenth century.

The 'Viennese' grand from c.1760 to c.1850

Sometime during the 1760s and 1770s performers must have begun to demand more flexible means of operating the mechanisms previously worked by hand stops. Instrument makers duly obliged by replacing hand stops with knee levers – these became the norm on German and Austrian pianos until they were replaced by pedals in the early years of the nineteenth century. The transition can be seen at a relatively late date on the pianos of Anton Walter, one of whose instruments Mozart owned. A piano of Walter's dated c.1778 has three hand stops, two for raising the dampers and one for the moderator (the device which interposes a strip of fabric between the hammers and strings). Mozart's piano (early 1780s) has the same three hand stops, but in addition has two knee levers which perform the same function as the two damper-raising stops.[19] Whether it was Mozart who requested the inclusion of the knee levers, or whether Walter took the decision, is unclear; but the vestigial remains of the hand stop system suggest that this is a transitional design. An additional curiosity is the way in which the right knee lever overlaps the left: it is possible to raise the bass dampers independently of the treble, but not *vice versa*. Later eighteenth-century pianos by Walter seem to have a 'standard' disposition of two knee levers, one for the dampers and one for the moderator.[20]

Walter's pianos were acknowledged in their day to be among the best available.[21] Walter's chief rival was Stein, several of whose instruments survive. The standard arrangement on these instruments from the 1770s to the 1790s is different from Walter's. Instead of knee levers for moderator and damper raising there are usually two for lifting the dampers, but no moderator. These levers operate each end of the damper rail so that it is possible to raise either the treble or bass dampers, or all of them. As on Walter's pianos, the damper rail is undivided, so that there is no clear division between treble and bass dampers (unlike the English system, in which the damper rail was sometimes cut in two around middle C). The distinction between treble and bass damping is consequently not at all precise.

Other makers generally followed one of these two 'standard' arrangements or something more or less equivalent to them. It can therefore be assumed that almost any grand piano appropriate to the mature Haydn/Mozart and early Beethoven period would have either one or two sustaining levers with the probable addition of a moderator lever or stop. Other types of soft pedal seem rarely, if ever, to have been used on the 'Viennese' piano in the eighteenth century.

The beginning of the nineteenth century saw two important developments; the disappearance of knee levers in favour of pedals and an increase in the standard number of devices on grand pianos. Certain makers evidently continued to use knee levers after others had already made the transition to pedals. No precise transitional date can therefore be identified. A number of pianos with knee levers exist from the first three or four years of the nineteenth century, whilst most after c.1810 seem to have been made with pedals. It is reasonable to assume, therefore, that the transition took place during the period c.1805–10.

At the same time, the number of devices increased, though a small number of instruments before the turn of the century had already incorporated an additional lever (usually the bassoon).[22] The una corda was introduced in the early years of the nineteenth century (see Chapter 9), and after c.1805 it was the norm for the 'Viennese' piano to have four or five pedals. Graf (1782–1851) was a particularly popular maker, whose pianos were played by many of the important virtuosi of the early nineteenth century.[23] His early instruments (up to about 1820) have five pedals: una corda, bassoon, two degrees of moderator, sustaining. From then until 1835, the standard disposition is reduced to four pedals: una corda, bassoon, moderator, sustaining. For four years or so after that, the bassoon was replaced by a second moderator and in 1839 the number of pedals was reduced to three (una corda, moderator, sustaining), which is the arrangement found on Graf's last-known piano. No doubt some variation did occur, as on Beethoven's piano (1826) which only has three pedals (the bassoon is omitted). Schumann, on the other hand, seems to have been content to accept the standard four-pedal arrangement on his 1839 model. Only two of Graf's extant pianos have the sixth, 'Turkish music' pedal. This comprised 'triple brass bells, a brass rod to strike the lowest 16–18 strings, and a padded lever to drum on the underside of the soundboard'.[24]

Graf is a useful maker to consider because of the consistency of his piano design and the large number of his extant instruments, but similar trends can be seen in other makers too. The Streicher firm (successors to Stein), like Graf, included five pedals on pianos until about 1818. Unlike Graf, however, the fifth device was often (if not always) a Turkish music pedal (or in one case, a single knee lever). From c.1819, a four-pedal arrangement is common (una corda, bassoon, moderator, sustaining), but as with Graf, the bassoon pedal was dropped in the mid 1830s. Finally, at the beginning of the 1840s, the two-pedal pattern common on modern grands emerged.

Graf and Streicher between them are sufficient to demonstrate a clear trend in the design of Viennese grands during the first part of the nineteenth century. Other firms largely followed suit with the exception of a few rather extravagant makers such as Haschka (Vienna), who seems to have specialised in instruments with up to seven or eight pedals. These large numbers are achieved by taking Graf's five-pedal design and adding to it various Turkish elements, with different pedals to operate the drum, bells/cymbal and triangle. These instruments, despite their splendid appearance, are far from typical, and most probably not the sort that a professional musician would have owned (see Chapter 9).

German and Austrian squares from c.1760 to c.1850

It is very difficult to generalise about the design of square pianos; there does not seem to be the same degree of standardisation in their disposition as there is with grands. Cost was probably an important factor: cheaper square pianos not only were made of poorer materials but also tended to have the bare minimum of stops, levers or pedals. It should also be mentioned here that the square piano does not seem to have had the same importance in Germany and Austria as it did in the French and English markets.

The design of square pianos tended to follow that of grands when it came to devices for modifying the sound, although it sometimes took longer for squares to incorporate new developments. Baumann's squares, for example, normally had a sustaining stop, but only included a moderator after c.1780.[25] It is unusual to find square pianos by any maker before 1780 with knee levers; indeed some continued to have hand stops to quite a late date. Ignaz Kober, for example, began to use knee levers on grands by about 1780, but a square of his dated 1788 (now in the Kunsthistorisches Museum, Vienna) has just two hand stops. There is even a square by Schmal and Son dated c.1792 in the Schweizerisches Landesmuseum, Zurich, with five hand stops.

Pedals were used on squares in the early nineteenth century, but they were normally fewer in number than on contemporary grands. Most frequently there are just two – sustaining and some sort of soft pedal. The soft pedal (or stop or lever) might be a moderator, but it is more often than not a lute (also known as 'harp' or 'buff': a strip of leather or cloth which dulled the strings' vibrations). The una corda was almost impossible to fit on square pianos and is virtually never encountered.

The grand piano in England c.1760–c.1850

The design of grand pianos is much easier to trace in England than elsewhere. From 1772, the date of the earliest extant grand by Backers (now in the Russell Collection, Edinburgh), to the middle of the nineteenth century and beyond the standard design included two pedals – the sustaining pedal and the una corda pedal. Nevertheless, there were some exceptions: certain makers added various third pedals from time to time.

The una corda pedal offers a straightforward choice of one or both strings on the Backers grand of 1772 (which is bichord throughout). On slightly later, trichord, English grands there is usually a device at the right-hand end of the keyboard which controls the extent of the shift – reducing it from three to one or two strings, depending on the position of a small block of wood. This device lasted into the 1830s,[26] after which the real una corda became impossible, as it is on modern grands where space permits the keyboard to shift only as far as the two-string position.

The sustaining pedal was modified by Broadwood at the beginning of the nineteenth century. About 1806 the firm began to make grands with three pedals – two for sustaining and one for una corda. On these instruments the damper rail was divided around middle C (unlike continental instruments where the damper rail remained undivided) so that the treble and bass dampers could be raised separately. This arrangement made it impossible for the performer to raise all the dampers and use the una corda at the same time, so a couple of years later the firm reverted to the two-pedal arrangement, except that the right pedal was now divided in half so that this single pedal performed the same function as the two sustaining pedals on the three-pedal models. The new disposition lasted well into the early 1820s (Beethoven's Broadwood of 1817 had one): but it seems that the occasional three-pedal model was also being made as late as 1819.[27] A few other makers imitated the split pedal design. A grand by Tomkinson in the Victoria and Albert Museum has one, though it may be that the instrument was made in Broadwood's factory and sold under a different name.

Clementi's grands had an additional pedal in the form of the harmonic swell for a few years around 1820. This device controlled sympathetic vibration, which enhanced the tone of the instrument.[28] It was of limited use, however, as were other pedals which are mentioned occasionally in the literature. Apart from refinements in the una corda and sustaining mechanisms, the English grand maintained the combination of those two pedals almost exclusively throughout its history.

The only other development concerning pedals on English grands was their position on the instrument itself. Backers had set the pattern initially by attaching the pedals to the front legs of the instrument (in the same manner as English harpsichords). This must have been rather uncomfortable for the performer and by the end of the eighteenth century makers were beginning to move them into the centre of the piano. During the first decade of the new century a lyre-shaped support began to emerge which gave the pedals greater stability at a time when their use was increasing rapidly.

The English square and other domestic instruments c.1760–c.1850

Compared with grand pianos, English squares were slow to acquire pedals (appearances can be deceptive here – some earlier models which originally had hand stops were later given pedals or even knee levers). What appears to be the earliest extant Zumpe square (1766)[29] has just one hand stop inside the instrument controlling the dampers; but Zumpe seems to have divided the damper rail shortly after this, and the other instruments that he made before his partnership with Buntebart (begun in 1769) have two levers to raise each part of the damper rail. From 1769 the firm adopted a standard three-lever arrangement: treble dampers, bass dampers, buff. This was to remain the disposition of many English squares into the 1790s with others varying the pattern only slightly – by omitting the buff, or having a single lever to control the whole damper rail.

A rather curious development took place in the 1790s. A number of instruments from this decade appear to have had no levers or pedals at all. This trend was short-lived, however, and by the early years of the nineteenth century a single damper-raising pedal seems to have become standard. Lid swells appeared on instruments from time to time – especially, it seems, on instruments exported to France (see Adam's comments in the Appendix) – but they are not sufficiently common to require consideration here. When cabinet and upright pianos replaced the square as the chapter domestic instrument the disposition was more or less equivalent to that on grands, with a damper-raising pedal and some sort of soft pedal.

France to c.1800

French pianists relied heavily on foreign imports for the last few decades of the eighteenth century. For most of the 1760s the relatively small number of keyboard players who performed on the piano would have done so on German instruments, which at this time were only equipped with hand stops. J. H. Silbermann's instruments were influential, and the only surviving grand of his, dated 1776 (now in the Berlin Institut für Musikforschung), retains the 'standard' two hand stops for damper raising and lute. The English squares that flooded the market from the late 1760s extended the possibilities only slightly and when French makers such as Mercken and Erard began to produce squares in the 1770s they followed English models.

The 1780s and 1790s must have seen a degree of variety in the various mechanisms available on grands and squares. Imports of English squares – with hand stops – continued, and a few English grands probably found their way into the market too. Meanwhile, French makers like Erard were abandoning stops for knee levers on their squares. Taskin seems to have followed suit on his grands as well as his squares, to judge by his extant instruments, which have two levers (damper raising with moderator on the grands, and split damper raising on the squares). Presumably when Erard began to make grands in 1796 he followed the English use of pedals; but no grands of his from the eighteenth century exist to verify this supposition.

The French in the eighteenth century, then, seem to have had a choice of the mechanisms offered elsewhere in Europe.

France c.1800 – c.1850

From the turn of the century (and perhaps for a few years earlier) French grands began to be made with four pedals, similar to the arrangement found on German and Austrian instruments (though the French anticipated them by a few years). Three of these pedals were standard (damper raising, una corda, moderator); but there seems to have been a choice of either bassoon or lute for the fourth. Sometimes, a knee lever was used for whichever of these two was not included as a pedal. A useful summary of the situation in France at the beginning of the nineteenth century is given in Louis Adam's chapter on pedalling (see the Appendix, pp. 170–1). For a decade or so from c.1810 all five mechanisms were operated by pedals but by the late 1820s the number of pedals had been reduced to two (damper raising and una corda), rather earlier than in Germany and Austria. This was to remain the normal disposition of French grands.

In many cases French square pianos followed grands in their increased number of pedals in the early nineteenth century. Squares with four pedals are common. Other, no doubt cheaper, models just have two – lute and damper raising. Louis Adam also comments on the various dispositions of French squares at the beginning of the nineteenth century in his tutor (see the Appendix, p. 170).

After c.1850

By the middle of the nineteenth century piano design throughout Europe had become more standardised than at any point in its history previously. The 'Viennese' action had all but disappeared, making way for the 'English' action in the majority of grand pianos across the continent. The stranger forms of the grand piano (such as the upright grand or 'giraffe') were fast becoming obsolete, and the upright piano was rapidly replacing the square as the normal domestic instrument. At the same time the number of pedals had been reduced to two (damper raising and una corda – or its upright piano equivalent).

The sostenuto pedal

The only significant departure from the two-pedal norm was the sostenuto pedal, which began to appear as a third pedal on pianos in the second half of the nineteenth century. Despite the fact that it was popularised by American makers, it was in Europe (especially France) that several makers first began to experiment with different mechanisms to solve what they perceived to be an inherent problem in the existing sustaining pedal:

however skilful the performers might be, a confusion of sounds which was very unpleasant to hear always resulted from the use of this [the normal sustaining] pedal. Not only was a prolongation of the notes obtained, but a prolongation of all the notes, to the extent that there was no difference observed in the various note values in these passages. All note values, whether minims, crotchets, quavers or semiquavers were prolonged indistinctly until the moment the pianist took his foot off the pedal;

and it follows that such a melody which was to be heard and to dominate by its long tones became weakened and covered by an excessive intensity of sound caused by the prolongation forced on the accompanying notes.[30]

This was the Parisian maker Boisselot's assessment of the situation, summed up in his patent for a selective tone-sustaining device in 1844, the first of its kind. Boisselot's pedal was demonstrated at the Paris exhibition in the same year. A certain amount of interest in it was expressed in the catalogue of the exhibition (with a description of its mechanism); but the inventor's interest in the device seems to have been short-lived. At the 1855 Paris exhibition there was no mention of any selective tone-sustaining device in connection with the firm. Indeed, Fétis, who reported on the event, had to be reminded of the inventor's name:

Mr Xavier Boisselot claimed for his brother priority of invention for the means put into use for the production of the effect in question.[31]

Meanwhile another Parisian maker, Montal, had exhibited a mechanism which was reported to be very similar to Boisselot's.[32]

Montal persevered with the device and exhibited it again at the 1862 London exhibition, where it was noted that 'the pedal requires some little practice to manage, but the effect is good'.[33] Thereafter Montal's efforts seem to have ceased: he made no efforts to patent the device, and in his book on he piano the 'pédale de prolongement' is only mentioned a few times (whereas another invention, the 'pédale d'expression', is mentioned at every available opportunity!).

Boisselot and Montal were not the only ones to address the problem of selective sustaining. Goudonnet patented a similar pedal in Paris in 1845, but it had little success because of its complicated mechanism.[34] Lentz of Paris divided the damper rail into several sections (an extension of earlier English practices) but the multiplication of pedals that this caused proved too complicated.[35] Zachariae adopted a similar scheme in Germany and promoted it vigorously (including an instruction manual for it), but it failed for predictable reasons. Schmitt noted, politely, that

possibly a greater familiarity with the Kunstpedal might have proved its limitations less irksome than they at first sight appeared, but all teachers united in agreeing that its management was too complicated.[36]

This is hardly surprising, in view of the fact that

The Kunst-pedal of Herr Zachariae of Stuttgart divides the row of dampers by four cleft pedal feet into eight sections.[37]

The history of the sostenuto pedal gained fresh impetus from American makers as they rose to a position of prominence in the late 1860s and 1870s. Steinway, in particular, presented European makers with several challenges in piano design, the more important features being the use of cross-stringing and the cast-iron frame. Compared with these innovations, the sostenuto pedal (patented in 1875) was of relatively little importance; but the firm's aggressive marketing policy and the consistency with which they used the device quickly led many to regard it as an American invention. Schmitt, for example, in spite of all his specialist knowledge of pedalling, wrote that it was 'first invented by Steinway of New York'.[38] This view gained sufficient ground for Chouquet to hit back in his report of the 1878 Paris exhibition, reclaiming priority for the French in the invention of the pedal.

European opinion was divided over the merits of the sostenuto, as it was over several aspects of Steinway's design. Some makers immediately adopted it: Chouquet singled out the Russians and Austro-Hungarians, but makers all over Europe used it, such as Pleyel and Wolff (Paris), Ehrbar (Vienna), Schiedmayer (Stuttgart) and some smaller Swiss and British firms. Others were opposed to it especially, it seems, in England. Broadwood's, for example, who had been so adventurous earlier in the century, made their position clear in a pamphlet dated 1892:

THE THIRD PEDAL for sustaining certain notes whilst the remainder are damped being of no value in the concert room, and liable to get out of order, is not adopted by John Broadwood and Sons . . . .[39]

Even Steinway's, no doubt sensing the ambivalence of the Europeans, did not include the sostenuto on grands made by their Hamburg branch.[40]

Twentieth-century opinion has remained divided over the sostenuto. Bösendorfer's began to use it after the second world war[41] and the major Japanese makers include it as a matter of course; but many European makers are no more convinced of its worth today than they were a hundred years ago.

PART II

Pedalling and the early pianists

3

Documentary accounts of early pedalling

As far as the mutations of the piano are concerned, we cannot praise instrument makers sufficiently for their unstinting efforts in recent years to introduce a large number of mutations into the instrument. But they have seldom been used sufficiently by players and thus resemble a fine collection of books that no one ever reads.[1]
(Milchmeyer 1797)

Since the pedals remedy this defect . . . it would be quite wrong to renounce their use. We know that some people, by a blind attachment to the old rules, by a proper but badly understood affection, forbid their use . . .[2]   (Adam 1804)

To begin with this use of the registers was decried as charlatanism.[3]   (Steibelt 1809)

Several other fruitless essays were made to improve the construction of square pianos; and under the impossibility of attaining it, recourse was had to an augmentation of the number of pedals, the object of which was to modify the quality of the sounds. But these factitious means of producing effect were held but in little account by distinguished artists and true amateurs.[4]   (Fétis 1827)

These writers were unanimous in believing that stops, levers and pedals had been viewed with scepticism in the early stages of their history. Nevertheless, by the beginning of the nineteenth century such devices had been more or less universally accepted as an important element of piano technique. This change in attitudes occurred at different times in different places, and was the cause of a debate which can be observed in a variety of sources. It is this controversy and process of change which forms the study of the next three chapters.

The use of stops, levers and pedals to c.1790

Keyboard tutors prior to the 1790s make no more than passing references to stops, levers and pedals. Our knowledge of their use in this period is therefore largely dependent on other sources, which unfortunately offer only the sketchiest

29

of information. It is therefore almost impossible to be sure exactly how pianists of that era used these devices. But from the information that does exist we can tentatively identify three factors which seem to have been important in the use to which tone-modifying devices were put to begin with: first, the ability which they gave performers to imitate other instruments; secondly, the way in which they helped the performer to overcome some of the short-comings of the early piano (such as its dryness of tone); and thirdly, their potential for novelty, or particular effects at strategic moments in the music.

Of these factors, the first (imitation of other instruments) seems to have been most important in the early stages of the piano's history. The instruments them-selves offer some clues here. Cristofori's pianos had an una corda mechanism which enabled the performer to imitate the changes in registration that a harpsichordist might have made. Gottfried Silbermann's pianos went further by including a stop whose sole purpose seems to have been the imitation of the harpsichord, by means of small pieces of ivory which could be brought into contact with the strings.[5] In addition, and for the first time, there was also a stop for raising the dampers (as on modern pianos), producing effects reminiscent of the pantalon.

'Pantalon' was a corrupt version of the first name of Pantaleon Hebenstreit (1667–1750) whose performances on his enlarged dulcimer (the 'Pantalon') were greatly admired at the beginning of the eighteenth century especially in Germany, but also in Austria and France. It was played with wooden beaters held in the hands and had no dampers. The effects produced on it were considered remarkable at the time:

Especially when one strikes a bass tone, it sounds for a long time afterward, like one that is held upon an organ, and many *passages* and *resolutiones* of *dissonantia* may be absolved before it fades completely – to the great delectation of the feelings . . . Nor does the harmony suffer by the pleasant after-humming of middle and upper voices, since even in the fastest things all notes are heard *distinctissime*. But when one arpeg-giates in chords – which can be accomplished here in the fullest manner – and since also when one ceases, the sound diminishes little by little as if from afar, the delightful buzzing of the harmony goes right into the quick . . . The instrument also has this privilege and property ahead of the claviers: namely, that one can play it with *force gratiae musicae*.[6]

Despite its capabilities the pantalon had two major drawbacks: it was expensive to maintain and particularly difficult to play. As a result the list of Hebenstreit's pupils is small: and because there were so few exponents of the instrument no music for it has survived.[7] Nevertheless, the curiosity value of the instrument ensured a profitable touring career for some, such as Noelli, who visited Italy, France, Denmark, Sweden and England. Noelli's career ended in the early 1780s, by which time the pantalon had enjoyed almost a century of exposure in the musical centres of Europe.

Schröter was the first to acknowledge the piano's indebtedness to the pantalon. He heard Hebenstreit play in 1717 and quickly set to work to make a keyboard instrument that would produce the same effects.[8] The result was two different actions: one in which the hammers struck the strings from below, the other a down-striking action. The second he called a pantalon, a name which was applied to many smaller pianos in Germany for the rest of the century. As late as 1783 J. Beckmann wrote an article entitled 'The Pantaleon':

Under this name are known at present two musical instruments, which, however, are essentially different. The one is that which is commonly and with greater propriety called the *Forte-piano*, or *Piano-forte* . . .[9]

The similarity between the two instruments was not confined to the hammer action. The pantalon's lack of damping was also apparently a feature of a number of early German pianos:

Though this instrument [the piano] met with general approbation, connoisseurs at first complained of the strong after-sound, by which the tones were rendered obscure and confused; but on this account artists more and more exerted themselves to remove this fault; and even Cristofoli [*sic*] himself found out a method of correcting it, by applying dampers to the hammers, which touched the strings with a piece of cloth as soon as they had been struck. A similar arrangement recommends those instruments of this kind, which are made by Francis Jacob Späth, an ingenious maker of Ratisbon, with the assistance of his son-in-law Schmal . . . By these means the forte piano is brought to such perfection that it is esteemed equal to the best clavichord.[10]

On pianos with dampers the mechanism for removing them from the strings was often referred to in Germany as the 'Pantalonzug'. Even in England, as late as 1788, the device was still being compared to that family of instruments:

By means of a slide which throws off the dampers the tone resembles a dulcimer.[11]

Meanwhile, in France, Dom Bédos had mentioned a similar effect:

When one wants to play the instrument without damping the sounds, to imitate the *Timpanon*, etc., one finds a register . . . by means of which all the dampers are raised so that they no longer touch the strings.[12]

A 'Timpanon', according to Castil-Blaze, is a 'musical instrument of the psaltery type. It is equipped with steel or brass strings which are hit by two small wooden sticks':[13] an instrument resembling, if not identical with, the pantalon.

Although a comparison was often made between the undamped register of the piano and members of the dulcimer family, other parallels were sometimes drawn:

In *fortissimo*, through the raising of the dampers, he leads us to believe that we hear an organ, the fullness of an entire orchestra. Now, in *pianissimo*, through the same means, he creates the most tender tone of the glass harmonica.[14]

– an effect much admired by Louis Adam (see the Appendix, p. 172 below).

It is clear from these various accounts that performances with the dampers raised were not at all uncommon in the eighteenth century – a fact which doubtless lies behind Adlung's and Hiller's otherwise strange comments (see below) – and it is also clear that some commentators viewed the natural state of the instrument as *un*damped:

Whoever dislikes the lengthy resonance of the strings can engage the dampers so that they fall onto the strings as soon as the finger is taken from the key.[15]

The instrument named *fortepiano*, that has been made so far by Silbermann only . . . seems most charming to most *Liebhaber*, especially when it is used with damping.[16]

C. P. E. Bach was more positive:

The undamped register of the fortepiano is the most pleasing and, once the performer learns to observe the necessary precautions in the face of its reverberations, the most delightful for improvisation.[17]

An actual performance with the dampers lifted was described by Charles Burney, who visited Paris in 1770 and was treated to dinner at Madame Brillon's:

After coffee we went into the music room where I found an English pianoforte which Mr Bach had sent her . . . she was so obliging as to play several of her own pieces both on the harpsichord and piano forte accompanied with the stops on – *c'est sec*, she said – but with them off unless in arpeggios, nothing is distinct – 'tis like the sound of bells, continual and confluent.[18]

This passage explicitly mentions Madame Brillon's reasons for raising the dampers – not, on this occasion, because she wanted to imitate the pantalon or glass harmonica. Rather, she used it because she was dissatisfied with the resonance capabilities of her English square piano – hardly surprising, perhaps, if she compared it with the much larger harpsichord in the same room. It is equally clear, however, that Charles Burney was not at all in favour of this sort of performance (his comments are all the stronger when one considers his distaste for the constant jangling of European bells that plagued him on his tours). The passage illustrates the differences of opinion amongst musicians in the second half of the century, and also incidentally suggests a flexible attitude towards the use of different keyboard instruments: Madame Brillon was content to use both the harpsichord and the piano.

The resonance problem was not the only one to be overcome by stops, levers and pedals on the early piano. The dynamic capability of the instrument could also be enhanced by certain devices:

The most beautiful [effect] is the alternation of forte and piano by means of a treadle, without the necessity of stopping the performance, since by means of a register, pieces of leather or cloth are pushed under the hammers.[19]

Why should a touch-sensitive instrument require additional means to create dynamic contrast? The reason is a technical one, neatly summarised by Closson:

In order to prevent the jack, by its swift action, from breaking the shank of the hammer and also to prevent the hammer from rebounding from the jack and hitting the string a second time ('blocking'), it is necessary to keep the hammer at some distance from the string. Therefore, in order to give the hammer sufficient impetus, the key has to be struck firmly, and time must be allowed to permit the hammer to fall back into place, which means that a *soft touch* and rapid repetition are both impossible.[20]

Some (though not all) early pianos were limited in this way and a lever or pedal no doubt proved helpful. With the use of an escapement and other technical refinements later in the century, however, the need for additional means of creating dynamic contrast receded. Türk recognised this in his *Klavierschule* of 1789:

The pianoforte has the appearance of a small harpsichord, but [the strings are] struck by small hammers. One can play weakly or strongly on this instrument, of which there are several types at present, as on the clavichord, simply by a strong or weak touch, consequently without the use of a stop.[21]

Even so, there were some who, through ignorance, wanted to persist in the use of some sort of device to achieve dynamic contrasts. William Dale relates an incident concerning John Broadwood and a customer:

In the year 1799 a customer writes to Shudi's successor to have a Venetian swell put to a grand he has ordered . . . Before putting the swell to the piano the maker writes: 'If the gentleman who wants the grand pianoforte is not positive in having a swell, we would thank you to persuade him off it, as it is a thing that adds much to the intricacy and weight of the instrument, and is of no advantage, the forte in the grand piano being designed to be made with the finger, and not with the foot like the harpsichord.'[22]

Late eighteenth-century audiences enjoyed programmes which included novelty – Dussek's performances on the glass harmonica, or Steibelt's wife with her tambourine, for example. Similarly, music journals were quick to report the latest inventions of instrument makers, such as Taskin's use of soft leather (*peau de buffle*) plectra on the harpsichord. Novelty was evidently an important ingredient of musical life in the eighteenth century. Not surprisingly, therefore, some instrument makers included extravagant numbers of tone-modifying devices on their instruments, which certain performers were quick to take advantage of. None of the various keyboard instruments available at the time was exempt from the trend. In 1739, Blankenburg wrote:

in order to surprise the listener more quickly through unexpected changes, we brought the stops to the front [of the harpsichord], so as to be able to move them while playing with a touch of the hand.[23]

Later in the century Erard

invented the organized pianoforte with two keyboards, one for the piano and the other for the organ. The success of this instrument in the higher ranks of society was prodigious. The Queen commanded one to be made for her own use, and in the construction of it Erard introduced several novel contrivances, which at that time awakened much interest.[24]

Milchmeyer, a great champion of pianoforte pedals (see Chapter 4), was also the inventor of the harpsichord with 'two hundred and fifty changes of tone colour', mentioned in Chapter 2. The instrument received a favourable review in Cramer's *Magazin der Musik*.[25]

Despite the interest of a few writers, musicians in general seldom expressed enthusiasm for this proliferation of devices on whatever keyboard instrument. Petri thought that 'registers were seldom good' on the clavichord.[26] Reichardt scorned them:

All newly-invented *Claviere* with 6 and 12 different stops are patchwork and child's play against a Silbermann clavichord.[27]

Hüllmandel, commenting on effects such as the mandolin, lute, harp, bassoon and oboe which had become possible on the harpsichord, wrote:

Are we tied to this instrument by such false and puerile imitations [imitative stops]? There is an instrument that far better fulfils the purpose of music and possesses evenness and purity of sound in any desired degree of strength or sweetness and speaks to the heart without hurting the ear.[28]

He was, of course, defending the pianoforte.

Although it lies outside the scope of the present section, a rather startling account of an American lady nevertheless illustrates the lengths to which some performers went in their pursuit of novelty:

There is an Astor piano in Salem . . . made as late as 1815. It had two pedals, one being used to prolong the tones. The other served to produce a novel and taking effect, by lifting a section of the top of the piano lid, which was then allowed to fall suddenly, the slamming serving to illustrate the firing of cannon. The young lady who owned the piano created a sensation by playing battle pieces with this startling accompaniment.[29]

No doubt there were a few in the eighteenth century who were similarly prepared to plumb the depths of bad taste.

National styles

The instruments of Vienna and London have produced two different schools. The pianists of Vienna are especially distinguished for the precision, clearness and rapidity of their execution; the instruments fabricated in that city are extremely easy to play, and, in order to avoid confusion of sound, they are made with mufflers up to the last high note; from this results a great dryness in sostenuto passages, as one sound does not flow into another. In Germany the use of the pedals is scarcely known. English pianos possess rounder sounds and a somewhat heavier touch; they have caused the professors of that country to adopt a grander style, and that beautiful manner of *singing* which distinguishes them; to succeed in this, the use of the loud pedal is indispensable, in order to conceal the dryness inherent to the pianoforte.[30]

This was Kalkbrenner's rather simplistic account of European piano playing in 1830. It is simplistic for a number of reasons. It suggests, for example, that all Viennese pianists played very neatly; yet anyone familiar with accounts of Beethoven's playing will know that in the earlier years of the century he developed a much more vigorous style of performance which was followed by some other pianists. Kalkbrenner also exaggerates heavily when he states that the pedals were 'scarcely known' in Germany: much of the repertoire demands their use and there is ample evidence to show that pianists employed them regularly in performance. Nevertheless, Kalkbrenner is correct in pointing out general differences between performers on 'Viennese' and 'London' pianos; and these differences, if considered carefully, provide a useful framework for a study of pedalling. They began to emerge in the eighteenth century when the pianists of Paris, Vienna and London began to approach the pedals in different ways.

Paris

From the middle of the eighteenth century there is evidence that some French keyboard players used the stops, levers and pedals that had begun to appear on keyboard instruments. Jean-François Tapray and Armand-Louis Couperin, two well-respected Parisian musicians, both included directions for the harpsi-chord's knee levers in published words.[31] According to Milchmeyer, however (whose piano tutor was written following a twenty-four-year period of study of the instrument, eighteen of which had been spent in Paris and Lyons), the pedals had been ignored[32] until Steibelt's arrival in Paris – he settled there in 1790, having previously visited the city:

Composers and teachers ignored them, and regarded them as unnecessary, until finally the great talent of Herr Steibelt . . . developed all these mutations carefully, demon-strated the effect of each one and defined its function.[33]

Steibelt's concentrated use of the pedals is amply documented in the markings that appeared in his music from 1793, and he was quickly followed by a num-ber of others (see Chapter 5). Rieger summed up the position well in 1820:

Steibelt is the only author whose pieces have been composed expressly for the use of the pedals . . . many people imitated Steibelt's manner.[34]

Looking back on the period, Chaulieu expressed some reservations because of the use to which the pedals were put:

It was also at this time that the *tremolo* was born; the use of the pedals was pushed to extremes and, while one believed to have found a pedal imitating the harp, another proudly believed to have imitated the bassoon. This stupidity was then carried to its peak by the drum, bells, etc., etc.; finally, the craze became such that our children would hardly believe it.[35]

Not surprisingly, this sort of use of the pedals had plenty of critics at the time, despite Steibelt's popularity with audiences:

If he had his ardent admirers, he also had his many critics. These reproached him for the immoderate use he made of the *tremolo* [which depended on the sustaining pedal for its effect] . . .[36]

Beethoven's reaction to this style of performance was highly characteristic when the two pianists met:

[Beethoven] went in his usual (I might say, ill-bred) manner to the instrument as if half-pushed, picked up the violoncello part of Steibelt's quintet in passing, placed it (intentionally?) upon the stand upside down and with one finger drummed out a theme of the first few measures. Insulted and angered, he improvised in such a manner that Steibelt left the room before he finished, would never again meet him and, indeed, made it a condition that Beethoven should not be invited before accepting an offer.[37]

Tomaschek was similarly unimpressed:

[Steibelt] did nothing other than repeat the C major *vibrando* theme a few times while running up and down the keys with his right hand, and the 'improvisation' was over within a few minutes.[38]

The craze for performance in the *tremolando* style seems to have been at its height around the turn of the century in Paris. It caused Louis Adam in 1804 to express the concern that more important uses of the pedals might be overlooked:

We know that some people, by a blind attachment to the old rules, by a proper but badly-understood affection, forbid their use and call it charlatanism. We will be of their opinion when they make this objection against those performers who only use the pedals to dazzle the ignorant in music, or to disguise the mediocrity of their talent; but those who only use them appropriately to enhance and sustain the sounds of a beautiful melody and fine harmony assuredly merit the approval of true connoisseurs.[39]

Yet within this passage from Adam's piano treatise there is clear evidence that some pianists were beginning to develop more refined pedalling techniques out of what might be termed, politely, the 'experimentation' of the 1790s.

Dussek could not have timed his return to Paris better. When he arrived there at the end of 1807 the quality of his playing was quickly recognised and appreciated all the more because of the excesses of the preceding decade:

Good sense and a great man did justice to all these ridiculous things [the craze for effects]; *Dussek*, on returning to Paris, demonstrated how all that pedal paraphernalia could only accompany mediocrity, a true charlatanism, and also that people did not know how to use the sustaining pedal . . .[40]

The *AMZ* critic went even further, elevating Dussek to the status of a reformer, when he reviewed a concert of Dussek's at the end of 1808:

Dussek, one of the creators of the true style of pianoforte playing, and now for almost a year again in Paris, made his appearance the same evening [as Rode] and charmed all his hearers, who apparently had come for the sole purpose of hearing Rode . . . Dussek had all the more brilliant success since for a long time no really great pianist had been heard in Paris . . . It was therefore most desirable that a man like Dussek should come here to reform piano playing and bring it back to its natural intents, worth, and characteristic qualities. Even in the first concert Dussek accomplished much toward this purpose, for he proved that success may be gained by character, simplicity, and grace, and that there is no need of the sing-song and little tricks used to attract attention to themselves by those who lack a sense of greatness as well as a really excellent talent.[41]

Not all the credit should go to Dussek, however. Steibelt may have been guilty of excessive zeal in his promotion of the pedals, but he was also praised for his pedalling on occasion by some of the severest critics of pedalling excesses:

He played the grand *adagio* from op. 64, during which he employed the pedals so well, of which the usage was little known before him.[42]

In his own treatise of 1809, Steibelt concentrated on a more serious use of the pedals:

A sure art of striking the keys and bending the fingers, a truly characteristic use of the registers (*Züge*) (mutations of tone by means of the pedal), otherwise little used and of which I was the first to demonstrate the advantages, give the instrument a quite different expression. To begin with this use of the registers was decried as charlatanism, and students disliked them; but those who outlawed them are overcoming their prejudice, while at the same time many of them do not yet know how to use these registers skilfully.

In the following I will show how this important addition to the instrument serves to bring out the colours better and to give light and shade to the performance, and that their use is subject to the rules of good taste.[43]

Whatever excesses Steibelt may have been responsible for in the 1790s, they certainly did not prevent him from developing his own technique in such a way as to enhance the expressive and textural effects in his piano music of the early nineteenth century.

The early history of pedalling in France was one of extravagance which gave way within a decade or so to a more sophisticated and, in the long term, useful technique demonstrated in the pianism of Dussek and the more mature Steibelt.

London

Kalkbrenner's account of European piano playing, quoted on pages 34–5 above, associated the use of the sustaining pedal particularly with the London school. A closer examination of the sources seems to support his view, but the evidence itself is not nearly as comprehensive as that for Paris during the same period. Ripin encountered similar problems in his work on the harpsichord in eighteenth-century England:

Unfortunately, there does not seem to be any English documentary evidence comparable to the advertisements that seem to have accompanied every new development in French harpsichord making at this period, and there exists neither an explicit English statement of the machine-stop's original purpose nor any clues to the date of its invention other than those provided by the instruments on which the device appears.[44]

Indeed, the only detailed reference to the use of a harpsichord pedal (apart from Mace's description of 1676) dates from the early nineteenth century. It is included in an article on the pianoforte in the *Encyclopaedia Britannica* of 1801 and whether it reflects the views of earlier keyboard players is not at all clear:

The harpsichord was shut up, like the swell organ, and was opened by means of pedals when the performer wishes to enforce the sound . . . the effect of the pedal on the harpsichord could not be mistaken; it was just like opening the door of a room where music was performing. Other methods were tried with better effect. Unisons were added to each note, which were brought on either by means of pedals or by another set of keys.[45]

Evidence for pianoforte pedalling is a little easier to find, but it is not without its problems. Most of the sources that mention pedalling explicitly are French or German and are two or three decades later than the events themselves. They are not, however, so far removed from events as might at first appear. Most of the pianists described in these sources were well travelled in Europe and would have been acquainted with some of the writers who described their performing styles in the 1820s and 1830s.

The London school of pianists was described by Kalkbrenner as follows:

Dussek, Field and J. B. Cramer, the heads of that school which Clementi founded, use the loud pedal, while the harmony remains unchanged.[46]

Czerny divided them a little more carefully, but failed to make any mention of John Field:

a. *Clementi's style*, which was distinguished by a regular position of the hands, firm touch and tone, clear and voluble execution, and correct declamation; and, partly also, by great address and flexibility of finger.

b. *Cramer and Dussek's* style. Beautiful cantabile, the avoiding of all coarse effects, an astonishing equality in the runs and passages, as a compensation for that degree of volubility which is less thought of in their works, and a fine legato, combined with the use of the pedals.[47]

Elsewhere, Czerny is rather more specific in isolating Clementi from the rest of the London school because the latter belonged to an earlier generation. One of the consequences of this, according to Czerny, was that Clementi did not use the pedals in his earlier performing career:

Mozart, Clementi, and their contemporaries could not have made use of it [the pedal] as it was not then invented. It was only at the beginning of this century that Beethoven, Dussek, Steibelt, &c. brought it into general use; and even Clementi has employed it very frequently in his later works ... It is not advisable to employ it often in the older compositions for the piano, as those of Mozart, Em: Bach, and the earlier sonatas of Clementi.[48]

Czerny was clearly wrong when he asserted that Clementi could not have used the pedal 'as it was not then invented'; but what would have been the source of this assertion? Did Czerny as a young protégé in Vienna hear Clementi play when the latter passed through on his travels in the early years of the nineteenth century, or was he relying on the evidence of Clementi's published music? The absence of pedalling in the earlier works could easily have led Czerny to his conclusion. The two pianists met in 1810, but by this time Clementi had been performing in public for forty years. Whatever his sources, Czerny's remarks are supported by at least two other pieces of evidence. Clementi's persistent use of the harpsichord when other keyboard players were already performing publicly on the piano (see Chapter 1, p. 13) suggests that he was not always enthusiastic in keeping up with the latest performance trends; and the nature of his early pedal markings (see Chapter 4) similarly points to a cautious approach. In addition, by his own admission, Clementi's style of playing had undergone some changes in the late eighteenth century. In 1781 he met Mozart and the two pianists were involved in a performance contest at the Vienna Hofburg. Mozart later described Clementi as a 'mere mechanicus without a farthing's worth of taste or feeling'.[49] In contrast, Clementi was deeply impressed by Mozart's playing:

I had never before heard anyone play with such spirit and grace. I was particularly astonished by an adagio . . .[50]

When, in 1806, Ludwig Berger (his pupil) questioned Clementi about the event, asking him whether he had treated the instrument on that occasion in his present style, he replied in the negative and added:

that in the earlier period he had taken particular delight in brilliant feats of technical proficiency, especially in those passages in double notes that were not common before his time, and in improvised cadenzas. It was only later that he adopted a more melodic and noble style of performance.[51]

Perhaps the use of the sustaining pedal was part of this new style.

Clementi seems to have been somewhat alone in his cautious treatment of the pedals amongst members of the London school. But what about the other members of the school? Perhaps most noteworthy of all is the inclusion of Dussek's name in the lists of its leading members. We have already seen how Dussek's use of the pedal was admired when he returned to Paris in 1807 earlier in this section, and there seems little doubt that he was one of the earliest masters of pedalling. He was in London during the 1790s, a crucial period for the development of pedalling; and the fact that his name was grouped with Field and Cramer suggests that they too were influential in this area.

Apart from these somewhat problematical comments about the London school, there is very little documentary evidence which gives us any insight into pedalling amongst early pianists in London. As far as we can tell, the worst excesses of Paris were avoided, although there must have been plenty of pianists whose techniques never reached the heights of Dussek's:

> One pedal is all that is necessary, namely, to raise the dampers while tuning. Many young ladies raise the dampers while playing, for the purpose of increasing the sound; they certainly succeed; and, at the same time, produce an abominable jargon, highly offensive to the ear; and, in general, a sure proof of the want of a good finger, and of judicious expression.[52]

Vienna

Kalkbrenner's assessment of the Viennese school's attitude to pedalling in 1830 was that 'in Germany the use of the pedals is scarcely known'.[53] This is both a generalisation and an overstatement; yet there is evidence to suggest that he was broadly correct in contrasting the technique of Viennese pianism with the London and Paris schools. Passions ran high on the subject. When Milchmeyer's tutor (see Chapter 4) was reviewed in the *AMZ* the fifth chapter, which deals with the 'Veränderungen' ('mutations') of the piano, was criticised particularly strongly:

> This must be the worst chapter in the whole work. The author recommends the pur-chase of small square pianos – why? Because there are more stops and mutations on them! He cannot praise sufficiently those instrument makers who put several stops and mutations on their instruments. Steibelt is the man who has shown the world how to use the stops! etc. No more need be said. We Germans would rather stick by our Stein instruments, on which one can do everything without stops.[54]

Later in the same journal, a similar view was expressed in a review of Boieldieu's sonatas op. 1 in which the only movement with pedalling, the slow movement from the second sonata, is described as 'insignificant' ('unbedeutend').[55]

Pedalling was an issue in the debate which took place over the different merits of Beethoven's and Hummel's performance styles:

> Hummel's partisans accused Beethoven of mistreating the piano, of lacking all cleanness and clarity, of creating nothing but confused noise the way he used the pedal . . .[56]

Hummel's piano tutor of 1828 continues this theme:

Though a truly great artist has no occasion for the pedals to work upon his audience by expression and power, yet the use of the damper pedal, combined occasionally with the piano pedal (as it is termed), has an agreeable effect in many passages . . .

He describes the 'confusion of sounds' which results from over-use of the pedals and continues:

Only ears accustomed to this, can applaud such an abuse; sensible men will no doubt give their sanction to my opinion. Neither Mozart, nor Clementi, required these helps to obtain the highly deserved reputation of the greatest, and most expressive performers of their day. A demonstration that, without having recourse to such worthless means, a player might arrive at the most honourable rank.[57]

Hummel's appeal to Mozart and Clementi is noteworthy. He was a pupil of the former and perhaps also the latter, though whether his comments should be taken to mean that Mozart and the younger Clementi avoided the pedals altogether is questionable. Hummel was not above stretching the truth a little in order to make his point. In his tutor, for example, he dismisses all 'toy' pedals such as the bassoon, harp, etc., as 'useless, and of no value to the performer or to the instrument';[58] yet only a few years earlier he had published a piece with explicit markings for the 'fagotto'.[59]

Hummel's use of the pedals was more restrained than most, however. Czerny may have been overstating the case a little when he commented that 'in Hummel's works it [the pedal] but seldom occurs, and it may generally be dispensed with',[60] since the texture of the music clearly demands it in many places; but a frugal use of the pedals is only to be expected from a pianist who exemplified the 'precision, clearness and rapidity of . . . execution'[61] for which the Viennese school was famous.

If Hummel epitomised the restrained nature of the Viennese school, then Beethoven provided the perfect foil. The difference between the styles of the two men has already been commented on, and Beethoven's music itself provides ample evidence of his keen interest in the pedals. There were few composers anywhere in Europe who marked the pedals so frequently as he did. Neither was he entirely isolated. Kozeluch, another pianist in Vienna at the time, demonstrated an early, if unsophisticated, commitment to the pedals. Referring to a set of three caprices (op. 44), he wrote to his London publisher on 24 January 1799:

On account of these three caprices, it is necessary to play from beginning to end with the open register. This register is called 'Die Dämpfung' in German, and in France it is normally called 'le Forte'. One finds this mutation on every piano. The mutation is raised with the knee, which produces the effect of a harmonica, because the sound is not damped and continues sustained.[62]

No doubt Hummel would have disapproved.

4

Early techniques of the pedals as described in tutors

The student of pedalling who turns to eighteenth- and early nineteenth-century keyboard tutors for advice on the subject is likely to be disappointed. In view of the great number of tutors published in Europe at the time it is perhaps surprising to find so few references to pedalling, and those that do occur are generally not at all specific about matters of technique. Indeed, before about 1820 only three keyboard tutors discuss stops, levers or pedals in any detail; those by Milchmeyer (1797), Adam (1804) and Steibelt (1809). Each of these contains a chapter or section on the subject which appears in translation in the Appendix to this volume. Tutors by several other leading pianists, such as Clementi, Cramer and Dussek, provide little information of any significance. This is almost certainly because of the market for which they were intended – the large number of amateurs who needed only elementary instruction, rather than comments on more advanced matters of technique.

In addition to material in the tutors of Milchmeyer, Adam and Steibelt a few scattered references to pedalling occur in earlier tutors. These are found mainly, though not exclusively, in German sources and a number of them have already been referred to in Chapter 3. They rarely exceed a sentence or two and never discuss technique in detail. Some conclusions can be drawn from their terminology, however, which is borrowed from that of the organ or harpsichord: *Register (Registre)*, *Zug*, and *Stimme* are the words most frequently used for stops, levers or pedals. Writers probably thought of these devices in the same way as their counterparts on the organ or harpsichord. Consequently they were to be used for whole sections of music, just as an organ stop or harpsichord register would be. C. P. E. Bach's reference to the 'undamped register' appears to make this assumption:

The undamped register of the fortepiano is the most pleasing and, once the performer learns to observe the necessary precautions in the face of its reverberations, the most delightful for improvisation.[1]

Because of the date at which this was written (1762) it is most unlikely that

C. P. E. Bach would have had anything other than a hand stop in mind here. This stop could only be released when one or both hands were not playing, so that large sections or complete improvisations would have been played with the dampers raised.

Other eighteenth-century tutors are even less specific in their discussion of 'pedalling' technique than Bach, with the notable exception of Milchmeyer, whose chapter on the subject stands alone as the only detailed account of the subject in that century (see the Appendix, pp. 159–69). It contains a comprehensive catalogue of effects and represents the culmination of a way of thinking that was described in Chapter 3. At the time of its publication (1797) there were no doubt many keyboard players who still performed in the way he describes; but such was the speed at which performance styles were changing that Milchmeyer's tutor was already well out of date as far as the most progressive pianists were concerned. They had already developed a more modern approach to the pedals, as we shall see in the next chapter when we examine the markings in their music.

Milchmeyer's comments on pedalling should also be understood in the context of his experience of piano playing. His tutor was published in Dresden (in German), but Milchmeyer had studied the instrument and its technique in France. There appear to have been relatively few grand pianos there, so it is hardly surprising that the author favours squares. Which particular instruments did Milchmeyer have in mind? We saw in Chapter 1 how the French relied heavily on imported instruments, yet English squares at the time had only limited resources of stops and pedals. Milchmeyer, however, states that square pianos had more pedals (or their equivalent) than grands: presumably he was comparing French squares with imported grands.

All of Milchmeyer's examples are designed for performance on square pianos, but he is careful to mark those which might also be played on grands. The first pedal that he introduces is the 'Harfen- oder Lederzug' ('harp or leather stop'; see p. 20 above), which was common on squares, but much less so on grands. Hence, examples which use this pedal are designated for the square piano only. The sustaining pedal is indicated by the direction 'ohne Dämpfer' ('without dampers'). Examples with this pedal could have been played on either squares or grands. The direction 'mit zugemachtem [or aufgemachtem] Deckel' ('with closed [or open] lid') refers to a lid swell which was apparently common on square pianos at the time. Similar devices were even occasionally found on English grands.[2] Hence, some of Milchmeyer's examples with this direction are designated for the grand as well as the square. The most perplexing directions of the chapter are those which are designed to be played 'auf einer [changing to zwei] Saite'. Normally these would be assumed to be for the una corda pedal of the grand piano; but all of Milchmeyer's examples with this direction are designated for the square. At first sight this would appear to be a mistake, since the una corda was virtually never attempted by makers of the square piano: yet the 'ff' indication next to the direction 'Auf zwei Saiten' ('on two strings') surely indicates that the full volume of the instrument is achieved on two strings. Since grands by this time were trichord it seems clear enough that Milchmeyer had the square in mind. Presumably, therefore, he had in mind the device on some squares at the time which effectively damped out the sound of one of each pair of strings – one which was rarely found on English squares, but which must have been relatively common at the time on French instruments.

The examples used by Milchmeyer to illustrate his remarks have a strong French bias. Almost all of them are from two works by Steibelt: the *6me Pot Pourri* and the *Mélange* op. 10 which were both published in Paris in 1793. These were almost certainly the first two works published with pedal markings and they form the basis for a lengthy discussion in the next chapter. The other examples are from earlier pieces by Steibelt (the originals of which have no pedalling).

The effects that Milchmeyer describes are almost always limited to imitations of another instrument or some other phenomenon. There are exceptions, such as his first example, which demonstrates how the 'Harfen- oder Lederzug' can be combined with the lid-swell for an ornamented passage. But he goes on to describe how the pedals can be used to imitate 'small bells', various vocal effects, the rising and setting sun, the harmonica, Spanish music (presumably guitar sounds), etc. For these examples to be fully effective they need to be heard for several bars to be appreciated and consequently there is little evidence of a technique in which the pedals are depressed for just one or two beats. The only exceptions to this are those examples which use the lid-swell for brief crescendos and diminuendos and one example where the sustaining pedal is introduced in the middle of a phrase and released shortly afterwards.

Louis Adam's tutor, published just seven years after Milchmeyer's, shows how much progress had been made in that time. There are still remnants of the old style, in which the pedals were thought of as means of imitating other instruments: Adam retains the designation 'jeu de Luth' or 'jeu de Harpe' and comments that it can be used to imitate stringed instruments, as well as observing that the 'jeu céleste' in combination with the sustaining pedal perfectly imitates the harmonica (a popular effect). What is new, however, is the care with which he begins to establish some principles for the use of the sustaining pedal, enabling it to become a powerful means of overcoming the 'dryness' of the instrument without causing undue blurring of the sound. Milchmeyer had already observed some of the difficulties involved in using the sustaining pedal, but he had offered little advice on its use. Adam, on the other hand, warns against its misuse in *fortes*, insists that it should be released before each change of harmony, and recommends its use for sustained bass lines and *piano* passages. His comments are designed to increase the melodic rather than imitative capabilities of the instrument.

Like Milchmeyer, Adam included several musical examples to illustrate the use of the pedals. A degree of inconsistency exists between these examples and his comments, chiefly over the harmonic clarity of the pedalling. His remarks in the text indicate that the pedal should be released and retaken at every change of harmony. The musical examples, on the other hand, contain a degree of harmonic blurring. In Example 1, tonic and dominant harmonies are apparently mixed for the sake of sustaining the low C at the beginning of the first bar in a manner resembling some of Milchmeyer's examples. Excessive blurring is

Ex. 1 L. Adam, *Méthode*, p. 224.

avoided, however, by the use of the 'jeu céleste' and a 'pp' marking. This is reminiscent of C. P. E. Bach's advice that 'necessary precautions' should be taken when using the sustaining device. It also resembles some of Milchmeyer's examples in which the harmony changes while the sustaining pedal is depressed, but where the music is played quietly, sometimes with the lid of the instrument closed or with the lute pedal depressed. It was evidently a popular style of performance which continued to be described in a number of early nineteenth-century tutors. Czerny mentions it even as late as 1838–9, by which time pianos had become much more resonant, and the attendant risks of harmonic blurring greater:

In passages which are to be played with extreme softness and delicacy, the pedal may occasionally be held down during several dissonant chords. It produces in this case the soft undulating effect of the Eolian Harp, or of very distant music.[3]

Both Adam's and Steibelt's advice on pedalling assumes the use of the French grand piano with its standard four-pedal arrangement (Adam had little time for the lid-swell on squares). In Adam's tutor significantly greater attention is given to the sustaining pedal, but in Steibelt's almost equal space is devoted to each device, perhaps reflecting his earlier obsession with novel effects. Nevertheless, in most respects his comments are similar to Adam's, but he does devote a little more space to an effect that was becoming extremely important in the piano literature of the period: left-hand accompaniment figuration in which the pedal sustains a bass note while other notes of a chord are arpeggiated or filled out in some other way above. This sort of figuration (which appears in music from the mid 1790s) was to prove decisive in drawing a distinction between piano and harpsichord music: it is simply not possible to make musical sense of it on the latter.[4]

Taken together, these three tutors by Milchmeyer, Adam and Steibelt give a fascinating picture of the developments taking place at what was arguably the most crucial phase of the history of pedalling. Their weakness, however, is that they represent the French school almost exclusively. English and German tutors, by comparison, contain only a very meagre amount of information on pedalling during the period. This simply underlines the extent to which the subject was something of a preoccupation at the time in France, whereas in the rest of Europe developments occurred with less fuss. Nevertheless, some significant information can be gleaned from other early nineteenth-century tutors.

Outside France, most tutors of this period, particularly the English ones, make at least some brief comments on pedalling. Whilst these generally amount to little more than a sentence or two, it is clear that the use of the sustaining pedal was quickly becoming an important element in performance. (References to soft pedals are relatively rare and will be discussed in Chapter 9.) Many of the references to it echo those found in Adam's and Steibelt's tutors: for example, Cramer in 1818:

The Open Pedal is chiefly used in slow movements, when the same harmony is prolonged.[5]

Even the conservative Hummel, writing ten years later than Cramer, recommends a similar technique:

its employment, however, is rather to be recommended in slow rather than in quick movements, and only where the harmony changes at distant intervals.[6]

The use of the pedal in slow movements was in large measure to enable the instrument to sustain melodies with longer note values (as both Adam and Steibelt point out). It was in this sort of writing that the piano's lack of sustaining ability was most apparent. Even in 1830, by which time piano manufacturers had made strenuous and prolonged efforts to overcome the problem, Kalkbrenner suggested extensive use of the pedal to compensate:

I recommend its use for all high passages; the vibration of high notes is so multiplied that the sounds always appear rather dry when played without the pedal.[7]

The use of the pedal to overcome this problem may well have been the reason why several European makers divided the damping mechanism in some way (see Chapter 2). Yet despite the popularity of this arrangement, evidence for its use is very rare. Only two tutors mention it, neither in a particularly helpful way:

According to modern fashion it is divided into two parts, the right serves for the Treble, and the left part for the Bass.[8]

Some of the most modern pianos have a division in the damper pedal (like the stops of the old Pianofortes) which raises the dampers from the treble or bass notes by pressing down the right or left side respectively. This is useful in passages where one hand only is engaged in playing as it lessens the vibration.[9]

Directions in the music itself are no more helpful. Only one marking relating to divided damping is known, but it is an instruction *not* to use the mechanism. Beethoven wrote, at the beginning of his sonata op. 53:

Nb. where ped. is written, all the dampers from the bass to the treble should be raised. O means that they should be allowed to fall back again. [Although Beethoven wrote this direction at the beginning of the first movement there are in fact no markings for the sustaining pedal until the final movement.]

Ex. 2 L. van Beethoven, Sonata op. 53, final movement

Why was Beethoven so specific here? The answer no doubt lies in the particular texture of the opening theme of the last movement, which requires the
use of the pedal for two important reasons; to sustain the bass C, and to sustain the long-note melody (Ex. 2). Each of these functions requires different
ends of the damper rail, hence the careful instruction.

Returning to the keyboard tutors themselves, little further specific information concerning pedalling technique is to be found in early nineteenth-
century sources. Tutors from the second quarter of the century onwards
explore the subject in greater depth, and their advice will be examined in
Part III. But before continuing to a discussion of pedal markings in the music
itself it is useful to consider two elements of our modern technique which are
conspicuous by their absence from the early tutors, in order to emphasise the
transitional nature of early nineteenth-century pedalling.

One of the most important aims of modern pedalling is to achieve maximum
legato, resonance and tone from the instrument. In a melodic passage with
simple harmonic accompaniment, for example, it is likely that the sustaining
pedal would be used with discretion to achieve these ends. Eighteenth- and
early nineteenth-century writers are similarly concerned that the instrument
should be made to 'sing', and recommended the sustaining pedal in certain
circumstances to achieve this end, as we have seen. Yet it is important to
note that the sustaining pedal was only one of a number of options. Other
techniques designed to solve the same problems could also be used. They had
been developed at a much earlier date on the harpsichord and clavichord
and lived on well into the nineteenth century.

C. P. E. Bach addressed the problem in the middle of the eighteenth century:

The keyboard lacks the power to sustain long notes and to decrease or increase the
volume of a tone . . . The conditions make it no small task to give a singing performance
of an adagio without creating too much empty space and a consequent monotony
due to lack of sonority . . . The deficiencies of the keyboard can be concealed under
various expedients such as broken chords.[10]

Spreading chords was a common feature of keyboard technique. It was
described by several writers, including Kalkbrenner and Czerny, who devoted
two pages to it.[11] Its decline coincided with the development of a more or
less modern pedalling technique, and it therefore seems to have been used to
a much lesser extent after the middle of the nineteenth century. In 1853, for
example, Karl Engel wrote of it in dismissive terms:

A common fault is the want of precision in striking octaves or chords.[12]

Another extremely important element of earlier keyboard technique which
created a fuller, richer sound was the practice of holding notes down longer
than their written duration. C. P. E. Bach described it briefly:[13]

The slurred tones of broken chords are held in the manner of Figure 168.

Ex. 3

Louis Adam's description is more detailed[14]:

When the highest notes form a melody in those places where there is a slur, and if the notes that accompany the melody form a chord, all the notes may then be held under the fingers, as long as the same chord lasts, as follows:

Ex. 4

This joining of chords must be applied to bass lines in the opposite sense, that is to say that if the left hand has broken chords and there is a slur, it should be executed as follows:

Ex. 5

By Moscheles' time, the effect seems to have become less popular[15]:

The finger must give to each note its exact value in reference to the general time of the piece, by not quitting the key until the next finger is in the act of pressing down the succeeding key at which moment it must be taken off.

Exception This rule need not be so rigidly observed when a succession of notes belongs to the same harmony; because in this case no mixture of dissonant sounds can arise . . .

Ex. 6

The author cannot too strongly enforce a judicious use of the above exception, because, if a writer wishes to produce such an effect, he has other means of intelligibly expressing it.

Ex. 7

Like broken chords, this technique seems to have become less popular at the same time as pedalling techniques were becoming more sophisticated. In 1853, Engel observed:

Some pianists are . . . inclined to hold one or other note longer than is indicated . . . which must be avoided.[16]

The second, and somewhat incidental, aspect of modern pedalling technique which the earliest pianists do not seem to have used concerns wide stretches, outside the reach of some performers. Intervals of a tenth, for example, which are not uncommon in the literature, pose a problem for some, though more so now than at the beginning of the nineteenth century (on some pianos at least), as Bertini observed in 1830:

I cannot resist naming also, another defect, or rather a little *ruse de guerre*, that some of the pianoforte makers have smuggled into circulation at the expense of sadly perplexing an unfortunate pupil, if he should have been guilty of practising on any other instrument than one of their last new manufacture. It has not, perhaps, been discovered by every one, that in order to admit the improvement of braces, (irons to strengthen the instrument) these makers have *increased the size of the keys* so much, that in one octave . . . many of the *new pianofortes are a quarter of an inch (English) more in extent than the old ones!*[17]

Not all early keyboards are narrower than modern ones, however, and other solutions needed to be found for wide intervals in the music. Adam suggested re-writing chords:

There are some passages with an extension which small or medium-sized hands cannot manage, and consequently execute; notes of intervals which are too wide must be omitted, while observing that the highest note of the right hand must not be omitted (because it is the essential melody note); nor the lowest of the left hand (because it is the bass note). The notes that have been omitted may be replaced at the octave, provided that they do not rise above the melody in the treble, nor descend lower than the bass.[18]

Clementi put forward an alternative solution:[19]

Ex. 8

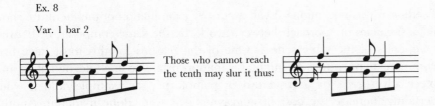

By Kalkbrenner's time, however, the sustaining pedal was used in similar situations:

Few hands are large enough to play a succession of tenths, but as these intervals are extremely agreeable to the ear, they are often employed for perfect chords in the left hand. The pedal must be used to sustain the low notes.[20]

These later techniques emphasise how much pedalling had developed in just a few decades. Techniques described by Kalkbrenner would not have been contemplated in the eighteenth century: they represent a very significant development away from the fingers-only approach of the early pianists. The period from the 1790s to the 1820s can therefore be regarded as one of transition in which conservative and progressive tendencies, along with personal idiosyncrasies, made for a wide variation in the practices of individual pianists.

5

Early pedal markings

Pedal markings occur consistently in piano music from the early 1790s. They were first used in France and within a few years were introduced in England. It took a little longer for them to reach the rest of Europe, notably Vienna, but they were common even there in the early years of the nineteenth century.

A study of these pedal markings is vital to our understanding of early techniques. They contain a wealth of evidence that complements the documentary sources. Even so, they are flawed in one important respect: they do not necessarily represent the composer's full intentions. Czerny, for example, noted in his discussion of pedalling that

BEETHOVEN, in particular, employed it in the performance of his pianoforte works much more frequently than we find it indicated in those compositions.[1]

Beethoven was not unique. Even a cursory examination of the literature shows inconsistencies of approach between works by the same composer, or between composers of the same school. One of the reasons for this must have been commercial pressures: it might be inappropriate to include pedalling in a piece advertised 'for harpsichord or pianoforte', for example, and it would certainly increase the cost of engraving if it were done in detail. Another reason was doubtless the thoroughness or otherwise of individual composers. Dussek, for example, was renowned for his command of the pedals, yet seems to have been remarkably lazy in providing indications for them. Several first editions of his works have no markings for them at all (the Sonatas op. 47 (1801) and the Fantasia and Fugue op. 55 (1804) for example) while others have only two or three (such as the Trio op. 65 (1807) and the *Notturno* op. 68 (1809)). Clementi, on the other hand, although a good deal more conservative in his pedalling, made extensive and careful markings for it: virtually all of his later works include numerous indications. Dussek and Clementi represent two extremes, but they illustrate well the problems associated with this kind of evidence. The modern performer should therefore be acquainted with the individual habits of a composer before making decisions about appropriate pedallings in his music.

The earliest indication for any tone-modifying device in piano music is found in the first sonata from a set of three dedicated 'à Madame Victoire de France' by Louis Jadin (c.1787). At the beginning of the second movement the direction 'con sordini' occurs. This is presumably an indication for the lute. Jadin would almost certainly have had a hand stop mechanism in mind with the consequence that the whole movement, or at least substantial sections of it, would be played on a new 'registration'.

Jadin's indication appears to be unique in the 1780s. The next example occurs, not in a printed work, but in a Beethoven sketch dated 1790–2.[2]

Ex. 9 L. van Beethoven, 'Kafka' sketchbook, folio 96r

Example 9 shows how the composer wrote the direction 'mit dem Knie' ('with the knee') underneath a series of chords with the purpose of sustaining bass notes longer than would otherwise be the case with the fingers alone. It is difficult to assess the significance of this example. Clearly Beethoven was taking advantage of the sustaining knee lever in a way that was to become extremely important to later pianists: yet this kind of figuration is not at all common in his earlier piano works, so that it is impossible to appeal to the example as evidence of an extensive use of the pedals at this stage of Beethoven's career. This sketch does not necessarily represent Beethoven's performance practice at the time, but it is at least evidence of his growing awareness of the potential of the sustaining pedal.

Paris

Steibelt and Boieldieu

Jadin's and Beethoven's markings are rather isolated examples; neither marks the beginnings of any observable trends. But in Steibelt's *6ᵐᵉ Pot Pourri* we begin to see the start of the Parisian fashion for pedalling that has already been described in Chapter 3. This work was advertised in the *Affiches, Annonces et Avis divers* on 7 March 1793, and was part of a series of similar works which are loosely constructed around a number of well-known melodies. It belongs to a

Ex. 10 D. Steibelt, *6me Pot Pourri*, frontispiece

genre that was becoming very popular at the time. Publishers and composers were not slow to realise the commercial potential, as Madame Pleyel illustrates in a letter to her husband:

We will do far better to print all sorts of small works every day, which require no great advances and on which the return is sure.[3]

The regularity with which Steibelt produced these works suggest that he too saw the financial advantages, and his name quickly became associated with the genre. Méreaux and Fétis both credit Steibelt with the invention of the pot-pourri,[4] although pieces with this title had been advertised as early as 1777, well before Steibelt's arrival in Paris. A large element in the success of these works was no doubt the ingenuity and novelty with which the various melodies were presented. Here, then, was the ideal place to introduce markings for tone-modifying devices. Their effects would enhance the genre, whereas their introduction into more traditional music, for example sonatas, was only likely to fuel controversy. Indeed, it was not until the Sonatas op. 27 and the Quintetts op. 28, both published in 1797, that pedal markings are found in works in well-established genres by Steibelt.

The markings in Steibelt's *6me Pot Pourri* are for pedals rather than hand stops. The two pedals required in this piece are the sustaining and the lute or harp. This combination, as well as the illustration on the title page (Ex. 10), and the mass market for which the work was obviously intended, point to the use of the square piano rather than the grand. The directions for the use of the pedals are given in words rather than symbols, such as 'la pédale qui ôte les étouffoirs' (sustaining), 'la pédalle [sic] qui fait la sourdine' (lute), and 'les deux pédales ensemble'. In the slightly later *Mélange* op. 10 by Steibelt (advertised in the *Affiches, Annonces et Avis divers* on 4 November 1793) the list of pedals is expanded and made more specific. The following instructions occur on the front cover:

⊖ 1re Pédale à gauche servant à imiter la Harpe ['1st pedal to the left serving to imitate the harp' – presumably the same as the 'sourdine' of the previous piece]

⊖ 2e Pédale ou Pédale du milieu servant a prolonger les sons ['2nd pedal, or middle pedal, serving to prolong the sounds' – the sustaining pedal]

⊜ Dernière Pédale à droite formant le crescendo de l'instrument ['last pedal to the right forming the crescendo of the instrument' – the swell]

The swell pedal, although apparently a new addition in the *Mélange*, may also have been used in the earlier *6me Pot Pourri* despite the lack of markings for it: Milchmeyer's use of examples from the *Pot Pourri* to demonstrate the swell pedal suggests that he might have seen the composer himself doing so.

The use of the pedals in the *6me Pot Pourri* and the *Mélange* is very varied. Sometimes, the pedals are used to enhance the effect of figuration that is also

Ex. 11 D. Steibelt, *6me Pot Pourri*, p. 2

found in earlier works. In other cases, new figuration is used and the pedalling anticipates important later developments.

In the *6me Pot Pourri* both pedals are used each time the opening theme recurs (Ex. 11). This was to become a popular technique, and it is found in many other rondo-structure pieces at the time. It was evidently thought of as a useful means of giving the main theme a distinctive character, especially when it is the only use of the pedals in the movement, as is sometimes the case. The best-known example of this technique is probably the last movement of the somewhat later Sonata op. 53 (the 'Waldstein') by Beethoven (see Ex. 2).

New textures are very much to the fore in Steibelt's *6ᵐᵉ Pot Pourri*, and although it is possible to find similar examples in earlier works, their frequency is greatly increased in the *Pot Pourri*. The most important example from a historical perspective is the use of the sustaining pedal to increase the range of left-hand accompanying figures. Steibelt himself saw the importance of this technique and singled it out for specific mention in his tutor (see the Appendix). In the *Pot Pourri* the left-hand figures cover almost three octaves (Ex. 12). This is a significant departure from earlier keyboard textures in

Ex. 12 D. Steibelt, *6ᵐᵉ Pot Pourri*, p. 6 (the sustaining pedal is depressed throughout)

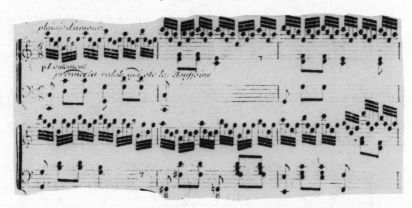

general, though it is not entirely without precedent: in the slightly earlier *Ouverture Turque* (1790) by Steibelt a similar, rather lengthy passage occurs (Ex. 13). There is no indication for the pedal, but it is possible to speculate that Steibelt would have used it here.

Another characteristic use of the pedals is in *tremolando* passages. The *6ᵐᵉ Pot Pourri* has a number of these, most notably a three-page passage which contains repeated notes, broken chords and arpeggios (Ex. 14). This proved to be one of the most controversial aspects of Steibelt's style, which attracted a good deal of criticism (see Chapter 3). Yet in spite of this criticism, it was a technique taken up by, among others, Beethoven, in the *Marcia funebre* of his Sonata op. 26. The *tremolando* is another technique foreshadowed to an extent in earlier works. Example 15 is taken from Steibelt's *1ᵉʳ Pot Pourri*, published in 1787. It is not such an extensive or consistent use of the texture but may nevertheless be an indication of Steibelt's use of the pedals before 1793.

The other examples of pedalling in the *6ᵐᵉ Pot Pourri* are less significant, but are used by Milchmeyer in his tutor (see Appendix, p. 163). The first shows how the lute pedal can be used for ornamented passages (Ex. 74) while the second apparently enables the instrument to imitate small bells (Ex. 76).

Ex. 13 D. Steibelt, *Ouverture Turque*, p. 6

Ex. 14 D. Steibelt, *6ᵐᵉ Pot Pourri*, p. 14

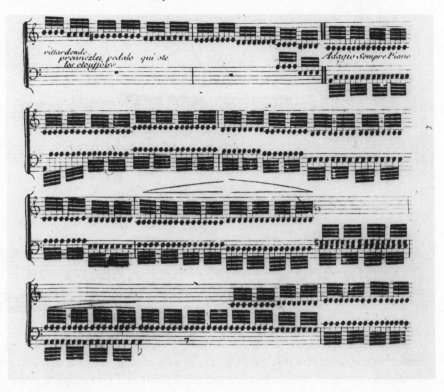

Ex. 15 D. Steibelt, *1ᵉʳ Pot Pourri*, p. 12

The pedal markings in the slightly later *Mélange* are similar in character to those in the *6ᵐᵉ Pot Pourri* with the exception of additional (but sparse) markings for the swell. The use of symbols rather than words to indicate the pedals is a development which was probably caused by the increased number of markings as well as their duration: the sustaining pedal, in particular, is sometimes used for very brief passages (Exx. 16 and 17), suggesting that Steibelt was becoming more conscious of the blurring of harmonies that occurred when this pedal was used. Nevertheless, there remain numerous passages where the sustaining pedal is depressed for several bars at a time.

Ex. 16 D. Steibelt, *Mélange*, op. 10, p. 4

Ø indicates depress the sustaining pedal

Ø indicates raise the sustaining pedal

Ex. 17 D. Steibelt, *Mélange*, op. 10, p. 8

The difference in the keyboard writing in these two works compared with earlier examples is striking. Steibelt was clearly setting out in a new direction – a comment that is reinforced by the somewhat self-conscious statement on the front cover of the *Pot Pourri* that 'this piece cannot be played without the pedals'. This is not to say that Steibelt himself was only just beginning to use the pedals. Some earlier examples where he may have used the pedals have already been suggested, and to these should be added examples from Steibelt's first and third *Pots Pourris* which found their way into Milchmeyer's tutor as examples of pedalling – perhaps reflecting Steibelt's own performances. Nevertheless, the markings that began to appear in 1793 represent an important step in the history of pedalling which others were quick to follow. Mozin, for example, quickly set about producing pot-pourris with lengthy passages of *tremolando* and continued writing in this style long after Steibelt had progressed to more interesting uses of the pedals.

A striking aspect of many of Steibelt's earliest pedal markings is their duration. This is not particularly notable in the case of lute or swell pedal indications, but those for the sustaining pedal are of interest since a number of them apparently leave the pedal depressed for several bars, or even several pages at a time. The problem is not confined to Steibelt's works: the direction at the beginning of Beethoven's Sonata op. 27 no. 2 ('Si deve suonare tutto questo pezzo delicatissimamente e senza sordini') which suggests that the pedal be depressed for the whole movement has perplexed generations of pianists. Did these early pianists really play whole movements or sections of work with the pedal depressed? Several factors suggest that they did, at least until the early years of the nineteenth century.

As we have seen in previous chapters, the existence of hand stops to raise the dampers on early pianos would have meant that pianists played complete sections or movements without the dampers. It is of course impossible to assess how popular this style of playing was, but there is evidence that at least some pianists liked the effect (see above, pp. 31–2). The fact that hand stops were common on square pianos some time after knee levers and pedals were regularly fitted to grands, however, suggests that it continued to be popular for some time. It is not unreasonable to suppose, therefore, that Steibelt's pedal markings indicating that the dampers be raised continuously for several bars should be interpreted literally. This view is reinforced by the specific way in which the pedals are indicated at some points in the score. Example 18, for

Ex. 18 D. Steibelt, *6ᵐᵉ Pot Pourri*, p. 16

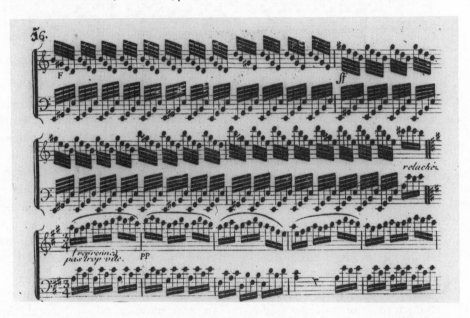

instance, includes the direction 'Relachez'. This is the indication to release the sustaining pedal, after three pages of *tremolando*. It is followed immediately by 'reprennez'. These two markings would have been unnecessary had the composer assumed that the pianist would raise and depress the pedal a number of times during this and the preceding passage. Rather, they suggest that Steibelt wanted continuous pedal through the *tremolando* section, but that he also wanted the accumulated sound cleared before the beginning of the new 'pp' section.

An even more specific example is found in the last movement of Boieldieu's *Premier Concerto* (Ex. 19). This variation has at the beginning: 'Grande Pédale

Ex. 19 A. Boieldieu, *1er Concerto*, p. 14

toute la variation. Sourdine aux accords seulement' ('Sustaining pedal for the
whole variation. "Sourdine" for the chords only'). It is not entirely clear what
'sourdine' would have meant here (the term can be used specifically, or simply
in its general sense to indicate some sort of mute). The work would almost
certainly have been played on a grand piano (a square piano would have been
most unusual for a concerto), yet which sort of grand is open to question –
probably one of French manufacture, but quite possibly an English or Viennese
one. The use of the 'sourdine' to highlight the left-hand chords suggests a
continental instrument, with a moderator or lute type of soft pedal, rather than
the una corda of English pianos. What is very clear, however, is that the sustaining pedal (the 'grande pédale') should be depressed constantly for the
whole variation.

These examples by Steibelt and Boieldieu demonstrate another common
characteristic of passages which require continuous sustaining pedal: they
contain safeguards against too much blurring of the harmony. Steibelt's piece
remains 'p' or 'pp' for much of the time, and where it becomes louder the
harmony is static. Boieldieu's lies relatively high on the keyboard where
resonance is poorer, with the exception of the left-hand chords, whose
resonance will inevitably be reduced, whichever soft pedal is used. Similarly,
the first movement of Beethoven's Sonata op. 27 no. 2 is to be played in a
very restrained manner, with a dynamic level which never rises above *piano*.

After this detailed examination of some of the earliest pedal markings, it
would be convenient to be able to follow the progress of composers such as
Steibelt and Boieldieu through a steady stream of works into the nineteenth

century; but in both cases there are problems which prevent this straightforward approach. Steibelt, having been so enthusiastic in the early stages, omitted pedalling from a large number of works from the later 1790s, including the majority of his pot-pourris as well as many more serious pieces. The reason for this is not clear: it may be that he found the inevitably increasing number of indications irksome to notate, or that his publishers were reluctant to go to the expense of including them. On the other hand, it may have become clear at an early stage that the precise marking of pedalling was very difficult – the exact way in which a piece is pedalled is unlikely to be the same in all circumstances, and will depend on the nature and resonance of the particular instrument used and a number of other factors. Some hint of a recognition of these problems is found in an indication on page 34 of the first edition of Steibelt's Sonata op. 27 no. 1 (1797), which reads:

Use the pedal that raises the dampers, but when you hear that the harmony is too confused, release the pedal for the value of a quaver and retake it immediately.

Boieldieu's music of the 1790s is a little more forthcoming than Steibelt's. Pedalling occurs in his *Premier Concerto* referred to above, which was composed in 1792 but only published c.1795, as well as in the sets of sonatas opp. 1, 2 and 3 (c.1795, c.1795, c.1799 respectively). It is also included in the Trio op. 5 but is conspicuous by its absence in a number of later sonatas (e.g. op. 4, op. 6, op. 8).

As a composer, Boieldieu tended to avoid the more trivial genres such as the pot-pourri, and instead concentrated on works for the 'quality market'. His pedal markings are therefore particularly interesting since they demonstrate the willingness of at least some serious-minded pianists to use the pedals. The markings themselves concentrate less on novel effects and begin to demonstrate elements of style that were to become important to later composers.

Ex. 20 A. Boieldieu, *1er Concerto*, p. 13

Ex. 21 A. Boieldieu, Sonata op. 1 no. 2, second movement

The majority of Boieldieu's pedal markings in these early works are for the sustaining pedal, which appears especially in slow movements. The *Premier Concerto* and the Sonata op. 1 no. 2 are good examples (Exx. 20 and 21). Both have slow movements (pastorales) which use this pedal, presumably to overcome the poor resonance of the piano. The Pastorale of the Concerto is just twenty-four bars long and bears the single direction 'Avec la grande Pedalle [*sic*]' at the beginning. It is followed by a series of variations the first of which simply has 'Sans Pedalle' at the start. The Sonata op. 1 no. 2 has a rather longer pastorale movement beginning with the direction 'avec la pédale'. Both pastorales are marked 'p' or 'pp' and are harmonically simple, suggesting that they should be played with the pedal depressed throughout. They are good examples of the type of movement discussed by Louis Adam in his tutor (see p. 171).

The Pastorale of op. 1 no. 2 also demonstrates Boieldieu's interest in the development of piano texture: the left-hand arpeggios can only be fully effective here when the sustaining pedal is depressed. A similar style is found in op. 2 no. 1 (Ex. 22), where the pedal is used in the middle of a faster movement (for how long is uncertain, as there is no indication for its release). The music is full of safeguards to ensure a reasonable clarity of harmony: the dynamic is again *piano*, the left-hand part is marked with a decrescendo immediately following the low F (presumably one of the main functions of the pedal here is to sustain this particular note), there are several rests between arpeggios in the lower (and most resonant) register of the keyboard, and the harmonic movement is slow. All this suggests that, as yet, the composer did not envisage a technique that would retake the pedal at every bar or half bar.

The slightly later sonatas op. 3 show no significant advance on the techniques described above. In the third sonata the sustaining pedal is used to expand the left-hand accompanying texture, but also to characterise the rondo

Ex. 22 A. Boieldieu, Sonata op. 2 no. 1, second movement

theme, just as Steibelt had done in his *6me Pot Pourri* (and Boieldieu almost certainly in the third movement of op. 2 no. 2, if the pedal is assumed to be released at the end of the theme).

Hereafter, apart from a single 'sourdine' marking in the Trio op. 5, Boieldieu appears to have lost interest in pedal markings. Yet it seems inconceivable that his pedalling technique did not continue to develop. The beginning of the first movement of the Sonata op. 6, for example, demands the sustaining pedal by virtue of its notation, and surely represents a more sophisticated use of this texture than was seen in earlier works: the pedal will need to be changed at every bar here, since the dynamic level is *forte* and the movement quicker (Ex. 23).

Ex. 23 A. Boieldieu, Sonata op. 6, first movement

For a more detailed examination of pedalling developments in the late 1790s it is necessary to turn to London, where composers began to indicate pedalling in their works shortly after they were joined by Steibelt in the winter of 1796–7.

London

Steibelt

The exact date of Steibelt's arrival in England is uncertain. Four works of his were published in Paris at the end of November 1796, but on 2 January his name appears in the books of Broadwood's firm in London and on 7 January *The Times* announced that he was to play in the first Opera Concert of the season (on 6 February), the first of a number of public appearances. It seems likely, therefore, that Steibelt arrived in London towards the end of 1796. He remained there until the autumn of 1799.

Steibelt had been in London for almost a year before venturing to include pedalling in English editions of his music. This was almost certainly a result of a conservatism in English musical taste which is also reflected in the choice of works that he placed before the public. He avoided publishing pieces of a less serious nature, such as his pot-pourris; instead, he chose more established genres, but even here he was selective. The first sonata of the set published by Imbault in Paris as op. 27, for example, was omitted from the English edition with the same opus number by Preston, presumably on account of its passages in *tremolando* style. Longman and Broderip eventually brought it out as op. 32, probably sometime in 1798. Likewise the *Caprices* op. 24, which had appeared in Paris in 1795, remained unpublished in England until 1798, presumably for the same reason. Indeed it is doubtful whether the *tremolando* style was ever accepted in England: Steibelt abandoned it after op. 32, and it is not found in any works by the other prominent pianists in London at the time – Clementi, Cramer, Dussek and Field.

The first piece by Steibelt to be published in London with pedalling was the Quintet op. 31 (advertised in *The Times* on 15 November 1797). This had appeared as the second of two quintets op. 28 in Paris sometime before and only uses pedalling in the *tremolando* theme of the last movement. It was followed by a few more works which had previously been published in Paris and in which no great developments in pedalling occur. Two other works, however, are much more significant: the last sonata of a set of six published by Imbault in Paris as op. 27, which nevertheless was almost certainly composed after Steibelt's arrival in England (the publisher's plate number for this particular sonata is much higher than those for the rest of the set), and the concerto op. 33, which was probably composed for concerts in the winter of 1798 but which was not published until the summer of that year. Both pieces demonstrate notable advances in pedalling techniques, which are best illustrated by an examination of the concerto.

The most noticeable change in approach in this work is the length of time the sustaining pedal is depressed ($\oplus$ indicates that the sustaining pedal is to be depressed, $\ast$ its release). Here it is used for short passages of half a bar or so, rather than the sections of eight, sixteen or more bars in earlier works. The by-now customary use of the pedal for extended left-hand figurations is exploited on several occasions (Ex. 24), and pedal characterises the main rondo theme of the last movement (Ex. 25). But the pedal is also used in new ways to enhance the tone of the instrument in its weaker, upper register (Ex. 26), as

Ex. 24 D. Steibelt, Concerto op. 33, p. 6

Ex. 25 D. Steibelt, Concerto op. 33, p. 20

Ex. 26 D. Steibelt, Concerto op. 33, p. 10

well as to add warmth lower down (Ex. 27). Elsewhere it enables the performer to play two chords legato (Ex. 28), though this example is not without its difficulties: either the release sign is misplaced here (which is not uncommon) or the performer needs to play sufficiently quietly and slowly to ensure minimum confusion between the harmonies, since the release sign occurs sometime after the second chord. Finally, the sustaining pedal is also used for dynamic accents (Ex. 29) and for creating an accumulation of sound in forceful passages – an effect which was easily abused (Ex. 30).

Ex. 27 D. Steibelt, Concerto op. 33, p. 12

Ex. 28 D. Steibelt, Concerto op. 33, p. 10

The increased complexity of pedalling in the Concerto demanded a new notation. Pedalling signs had been used as early as the *Mélange* op. 10 by Steibelt, but the particular ones employed in the Concerto appeared for the first time in the last sonata of op. 27. They also appeared very tentatively in the Quintet op. 31, but without any consistency: after an initial sign, the composer reverted to words (Ex. 31). In the Concerto op. 33, however, pedalling signs are used frequently, and with an explanatory note at the beginning (which was repeated in several other publications) which proclaimed Steibelt

Ex. 29 D. Steibelt, Concerto op. 33, p. 23

Ex. 30 D. Steibelt, Concerto op. 33, p. 26

as their inventor (Ex. 32). The wording of this notice is particularly interesting as it demonstrates the change in approach to the pedals that had been achieved by this time: it seems that they were beginning to be regarded as means by which the instrument's tone could be improved, rather than simply as novel effects ('The Author . . . finds it necessary to make use of the pedals, by which alone the tones can be united').

The reason for what appears to be a sudden development in Steibelt's pedalling technique is not clear. The sudden increase in markings may reflect the fact that almost all of his performances in England would have been on resonant grand pianos, as opposed to a wider variety of squares and grands of different types in Paris. The full tone of the English grand would have necessitated a more careful approach, in particular regarding the length of time that the sustaining pedal was held down. Yet this does not necessarily account for his increasing interest in techniques designed to *enhance* the instrument's resonance.

Ex. 31 D. Steibelt, Quintet op. 31, p. 15

Volti subito

Ex. 32 D. Steibelt, Concerto op. 33, introductory note

The Author wishing to make more Variety on the Piano Forte, finds it necessary to make use of the Pedals, by which alone the tones can be united, but it requires to use them with Care; without which, in going from one Chord to another, Discord & Confusion would result. Hereafter the Author in all his Compositions will make use of the following signs to denote the Pedals.

⊕ *The Pedal that raises the Dampers.*

△ *The Piano Pedal.*

✳ *To take the Foot off the Pedal that was us'd before.*

Perhaps this interest had been growing steadily over the preceding years without being acknowledged in the admittedly sketchy pedal markings of the mid 1790s. Another possibility, however, is that pianist-composers of the London school were already well versed in more sophisticated pedalling, without having felt the need to mark it in printed editions, and that Steibelt had simply learned these techniques quickly. This is suggested by the existence of a work by J. B. Cramer whose publication slightly predates Steibelt's earliest work with pedalling in England.

Cramer and Dussek

Cramer's second Concerto was advertised in *The Times* on 4 July 1797, four months before Steibelt's Quintet op. 31 with its rudimentary pedalling. The markings in Cramer's piece are rather sparse, but nevertheless show a degree of variety of sophistication which suggests that he may well have been using the pedals for some time previously. All the indications cover just a few bars or less and generally perform the function of sustaining a bass note while both hands continue to play in higher registers. But they are not confined to this single use: they are also used for *fortissimo* chords, arpeggio passages and short sections in the treble register. Whether or not they show Cramer to be more advanced than Steibelt, they certainly demonstrate that by this time the two pianists shared an equally developed technique.

Some writers have singled out Dussek from among the members of the London school as the pianist with the greatest command of the pedals. Gerig, for example, comments on Dussek's apparent innovation in placing the keyboard sideways on the platform and adds:

Ex. 33 J. L. Dussek, Sonata op. 39 no. 3, third movement

Ex. 34 J. L. Dussek, Sonata op. 18 no. 3, second movement

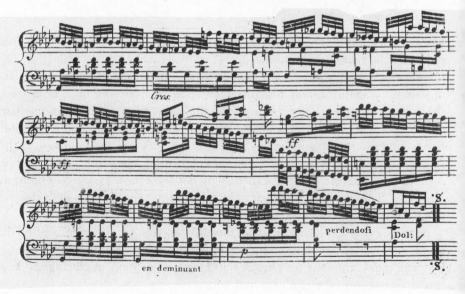

Other firsts for him include playing a six octave Broadwood grand before the London public in 1794 and also indicating pedalling in his own music.[5]

Harold Schonberg also places Dussek before all his contemporaries (including Steibelt) in his knowledge of the pedals.[6] Both authors may have been elaborating Kalkbrenner:

Dussek, Field and J. B. Cramer, the heads of that school which Clementi founded, use the loud pedal, while the harmony remains unchanged; Dussek in particular, was remarkable in this for he kept the mufflers almost constantly lifted when he played in public.[7]

But Kalkbrenner could have heard Dussek only when the latter had returned to Paris in 1807, and Field and Cramer considerably later than that (if at all), so his comments can hardly be taken as evidence of the situation in London in the 1790s. Moreover, Dussek began to indicate pedalling in printed editions slightly later than either Steibelt or Cramer, the first work being his *Military Concerto* op. 40 (1798). Nevertheless, the markings in this piece demonstrate a technique equal in sophistication to Steibelt's and Cramer's: the pedal is used

Ex. 35 J. L. Dussek, Concerto op. 29, p. 9

to reinforce the resonance of the piano's treble register, for crescendos, accents, arpeggios spread over a large range of the keyboard and for extended left-hand figurations. Of all these, the last two are the most important, particularly the left-hand writing, which had become a well-established element of keyboard writing by this time. Dussek's next works with pedalling, the Sonatas op. 39, contain some particularly wide-ranging examples (Ex. 33).

In view of the maturity of Dussek's pedalling technique in the *Military Concerto* and the Sonatas op. 39, it is inconceivable that he had not already been using the pedals for some time previously. Yet evidence for this suggestion is not easy to find in earlier works – much harder than in Steibelt's case. In particular, left-hand figurations rarely exceed the interval of a ninth or tenth in range, although there are exceptions. In the slow movement of the third sonata from op. 18 (c.1792) the left-hand octaves at the beginning of the bar will be cut very short without the sustaining pedal (Ex. 34). Likewise, the left-hand parts from the Concerto op. 29 (1795) and the third sonata from op. 35 require the pedal for a literal rendering of the notation by all but the largest of hands (Exx. 35 and 36). Other examples where the notation requires the

Ex. 36 J. L. Dussek, Sonata op. 35 no. 3, second movement

Ex. 37 J. L. Dussek, Prelude op. 31 no. 3

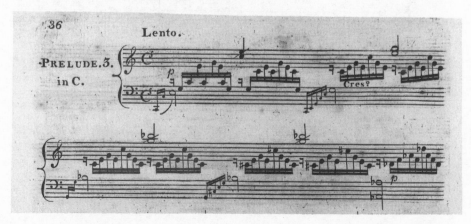

Ex. 38 M. Clementi, Sonata op. 37 no. 1, first movement

Ex. 39 M. Clementi, Sonata op. 37 no. 3, third movement

pedal for a literal performance are found in op. 7 (1789) and op. 9 (c.1789); and the Prelude from op. 31 would surely sound rather peculiar without the pedal to sustain the arpeggios in small notes (Ex. 37). But this is the sum total of the evidence to suggest Dussek's earlier use of the pedal. It is suggestive, but not very conclusive, and gives very little idea of the precise time at which he began to use the pedals regularly in performance.

Steibelt, Cramer and Dussek together illustrate the advances of the London school, which deservedly earned them the reputation of being among the most innovative exponents of the pedals in their generation (see above, p. 38). It is therefore particularly unfortunate that all three composers became so incon-

Ex. 40 M. Clementi, Waltzes op. 38 no. 7

Ex. 41 M. Clementi, Waltzes op. 38 no. 9

sistent in their markings for them in subsequent works. Ironically, of all the
pianists of the London school, it was Clementi who was eventually to become
the most careful indicator of the pedals. Yet the 'father of the pianoforte' was
clearly much less comfortable with this new trend than any of his younger
contemporaries in that school.

Clementi

Clementi's earliest pedal markings are very sparse and rudimentary. They
first appear in the sonatas op. 37 and op. 38. Op. 37 has two instances (Exx.
38 and 39), repeated elsewhere in their respective movements, which require
the sustaining pedal to be depressed for several bars (the second characterises
the rondo theme in the same way as some of the examples examined above).
In each case the marking 'dolce' is used, the bass line is static, and the
harmony only rarely changes. It is difficult to imagine that Clementi had
used the pedal much before this. On the contrary, it may be that he included
these indications grudgingly, so as not to appear left behind by his younger
contemporaries. The markings in op. 38 are scarcely more adventurous. The
first is very similar to the op. 37 examples (Ex. 40) while the second briefly
adds weight to the F major chord for two bars (Ex. 41).

Four years later, however, in the Sonata op. 40, Clementi was more adventurous, although the markings are still not as numerous as in some of Steibelt's and Dussek's pieces mentioned above. There is still a tendency to depress the sustaining pedal for several bars at a time with just occasional uses of it to reinforce an accent. The most frequent use of the pedal in this work, and one which was to become a hallmark of Clementi's pedalling style, is to accompany quiet passages in the treble register of the instrument (Ex. 42).

One particular effect is missing from Clementi's earliest pedal markings; the use of the sustaining pedal to extend the scope of left-hand accompanying figures. A simple answer may account for this. Clementi had begun his career as a harpsichordist and as far as one can tell by the accounts, he had made his name as a performer in London on that instrument (see above, p. 13). It would be expecting a great deal from a performer with a well-established technique to adapt quickly to new practices, especially at a time when business interests were occupying more and more of his time. We should not be surprised, therefore, to see Clementi overtaken by his pupils in this way.

The evidence of Clementi's earliest pedal markings accords with the descriptions of his playing cited in Chapter 3 (pp. 38–9). It also fits well with his own didactic literature. The first edition of his *Introduction to the Art of playing on the Pianoforte* (1801) makes no reference to the pedals. It is only in the fifth edition of 1811 that they are mentioned, and then only in a single sentence:

Ped: signifies to put down the pedal, which raises the dampers; and this mark ⊗ to let it go again.

The later *Gradus ad Parnassum* contains some pedalling, but very little compared with the music of contemporary pianists.

Vienna

Chapter 3 described the controversy that existed over different styles of piano playing in Vienna around the turn of the century, Hummel representing one

Ex. 42 M. Clementi, Sonata op. 40 no. 1, fourth movement

'camp' and Beethoven the other. It is therefore potentially misleading to talk about the 'Viennese school', as if there was anything like a unity of performance styles there at the time. Nevertheless, the conservatives seem to have had the upper hand, at least for a while. This is reflected in the fact that pedal markings did not appear in music by 'Viennese' composers until just before 1800.

Wölfl and Gelinek

Wölfl appears to have been the first to use indications for the knee levers, in his op. 6 piano sonatas, published in 1798. There are just four markings. Similar indications are found in Wölfl's sonatas op. 14 (c. 1801), from which Ex. 43 is taken. Here again the sustaining lever is raised for several bars, and there is a slow harmonic rhythm and low dynamic ('Senza sordini' and 'Con sordini' were normal indications for the sustaining pedal in Vienna at the time).

In contrast, Wölfl's markings in works published after he moved to Paris (1802), and later to London, are much more sophisticated. Meanwhile, in Vienna, some composers still persisted in their conservative ways. Gelinek, another popular Viennese composer, included Example 44 in a set of variations published in 1809. This sort of elementary marking would have been unthinkable in England or France by that date.

Beethoven

Compared with these examples, Beethoven's pedalling clearly has much more in common with the Paris and London schools (he admired the music of the latter).[8] He was among the first in Vienna to include pedal markings in his printed works (for example in the concertos opp. 15 and 19 and the sonata op. 24 of 1801 and the sonatas opp. 26 and 27 of 1802), and his use of the pedals goes well beyond the rudimentary, even if there is insufficient evidence to suggest that his technique was as advanced as some of his northern European contemporaries. The sustaining pedal is often indicated for a very short period, such as the sforzando chords in the last movement of the second sonata from op. 27. Beethoven also 'borrows' effects from his contemporaries, such as the tremolando in op. 26. Nevertheless there are passages which seem to have more in common with other Viennese composers, such as the first movement of op. 27 no. 2 (Czerny noted a similar passage in the slow movement of the Third Piano Concerto, where Beethoven apparently kept the pedal down for the entire theme – see p. 137). A mixture of styles is to be expected from a composer whose piano style has so much in common with the London school, yet who preferred to play on Viennese pianos throughout his life.[9]

Ex. 43 J. Wölfl, Sonata, op. 14 no. 1, second movement

Ex. 44 J. Gelinek, Variations set no. 47, variation 7

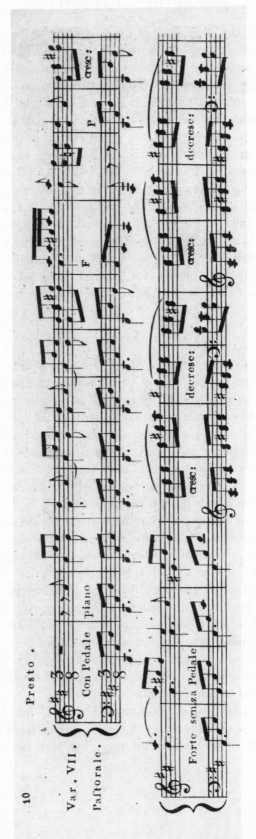

At the beginning of this chapter a reference was made to a very early pedal marking in a manuscript source by Beethoven from the early 1790s. At the same time the point was made that one such instance in a sketch could hardly be taken as evidence of Beethoven's consistent use of the pedals at that stage of his career. But the developed nature of his earliest markings suggests that he may have used the pedals in performance in the 1790s. In this connection Czerny's comment on Beethoven's style is both interesting and tantalising: he noted that Beethoven used the pedals 'much more than is indicated in his works'.[10] But which period of Beethoven's performing style was Czerny referring to? Was this something he observed as soon as he began his studies with the composer in 1801, or had he already watched him carefully in the closing years of the eighteenth century? These questions might appear trivial on first consideration; but the answers potentially affect a significant proportion of Beethoven's music for the piano (one third of his total sonata output, for example, and several other early works). Unfortunately it is impossible to answer the questions with any certainty.

Variable 'authentic' pedalling

Czerny's comments on Beethoven raise a wider issue of performance practice; is there just one style of pedalling (and performance in general) appropriate to any particular work, or is it possible to envisage a wide variety of 'legitimate' renderings? After all, a composer such as Beethoven would have expected his works to be played throughout his lifetime, during which his own style of performance may have changed radically. The problem is illustrated very clearly in the case of Clementi, some of whose earlier music was issued in new but authentic editions several decades after the works first appeared.

The longest period to elapse between first and last editions occurs in the case of Clementi's op. 2 sonatas. They were originally published in 1779, but appeared half a century later, in 1818 or 1819, in a revised edition which includes pedalling.[11] Other revisions of Clementi's earlier works appear in his Appendix op. 43 (1811) to the Introduction and in volume 6 of the *Oeuvres Complètes* published by Breitkopf & Härtel in 1804 (the only volume of his complete works to include substantial revisions). Well over half of the music in these collections which was originally published in the eighteenth century has pedalling added, mainly in places where a slur existed previously as well as in broken-chord or arpeggio passages. The later editions represent a transition from the finger-legato of the eighteenth century to a legato produced by the sustaining pedal.

Clementi was by no means the only composer to revise the performance directions of his works. A similar case exists in one of Steibelt's works, over a much shorter period of time. Steibelt's Sonata op. 32 was published by

Longman and Broderip, probably in 1798 as a copy of the French edition from the year before. It originally had just one pedal marking: 'Servez vous de la pedale qui leves Etouffoins [*sic*]' on page 2. But a slightly later edition published by Broderip and Wilkinson, successors to Longman and Broderip after the firm's bankruptcy in 1798, uses many of the plates from the earlier edition, but has several new pedalling indictions squeezed in. At the top of the first page the new directions appear:

⊕   the Pedal that raises the dampers

⟰   the Piano Pedal

✳   to take the foot off the pedal that was us'd before.

In the music itself there are many new indications, as well as an increased number of dynamic markings.

What is the significance of these examples? One thing at least is clear: the composers themselves allowed for a number of different styles of performance of their own works. It is possible, however, to go a little further. Alterations to pedalling would have been made in response to other changes in the circumstances of performance; more resonant pianos, for example, made a more 'singing', or legato, style possible, but equally made pedalling more hazardous. In the circumstances, a logical conclusion would be to match the performance style of any work to the instrument used on a particular occasion.

Because of the wealth of extant first editions of late eighteenth-century music it is possible to trace the development of pedalling from the experiments and effects of the early 1790s to something approaching the beginnings of a modern technique around the turn of the century. The significance of these developments were far-reaching: not only did pedalling styles change radically, but the way in which composers wrote for the keyboard was revolutionised. As a result, by the closing years of the eighteenth century the harpsichord was made obsolete for the performance of the most up-to-date keyboard music. There remain, however, areas of uncertainty. Did performers such as C. P. E. and J. C. Bach, Mozart and others use the pedals (or their equivalents), and if so, how much and in what circumstances? In the light of the evidence in this and earlier chapters it is at least possible to make some informed suggestions. These form the substance of the next chapter.

6

Mozart and his contemporaries

Having examined the development of pedalling in the preceding chapters we must now return to perhaps the most difficult area of all: the way in which first-generation pianists used stops, levers and pedals. The problem is common to all those pianist-composers who were writing music for the new instrument from the middle of the eighteenth century until the appearance of pedal markings in the 1790s. For the modern pianist it is probably most acute in Mozart's case because of his central position in the repertoire, and it is his music that will chiefly occupy us here. Certain questions that arise in the course of this discussion will nevertheless be relevant to the works of his contemporaries, some of whose music is discussed in detail at the end of this chapter.

Mozart

There are no indications of any sort for stops, levers, or pedals in Mozart's music and only one specific reference to such a device in documentary sources. This is contained in a letter which Wolfgang wrote to his father on 17 October 1777 from Augsburg. It is a well-known letter in which he extols the virtues of pianos made by Stein, whom he visited on several occasions. The letter begins with detailed comments on the instruments' action and what appears to be a digest of sales talk by the maker who claimed, amongst other things, to expose his soundboards to the rain, snow and sun so that they could crack and be glued before he inserted them into an instrument. Wolfgang then goes on to describe the earlier events of the day – lunch with Herr Gassner and another visit to Stein. The letter continues:

Here, and at Munich I have played all my six sonatas by heart several times (K279–284). I played the fifth, in G, at that grand concert in the Stube. The last one in D, sounds exquisite on Stein's pianoforte. The device too which you work with your knee is better on his than on other instruments. I have only to touch it and it works; and when you shift your knee the slightest bit, you do not hear the least reverberation. Well, tomorrow perhaps I shall come to his organs – I mean, I shall come to *write about them . . .* [1]

Several points arise from this passage. First, Mozart writes in enthusiastic terms about the sustaining lever. This would scarcely be worth pointing out were it not for those eighteenth-century writers especially in Germany who regarded all such devices as utterly worthless (see above, pp. 29–41). In defence of these writers, it is possible to speculate that stops and levers by other makers seldom worked well, since Mozart makes a point of praising the sensitivity of Stein's knee levers. Nevertheless, in this letter it seems that Mozart aligns himself with those more progressive pianists who were at least prepared to experiment with novelty.

Ex. 45 W. A. Mozart, Sonata for piano solo in D major K284, final movement

The context of Mozart's comments on Stein's knee levers is both interesting and tantalising. All of the other details concerning Stein's pianos are mentioned at the beginning of the letter, but his comments on the knee levers appear to come to mind as a result of remembering the way in which the D major sonata sounded on the instruments. Was there a particular pedalling effect in that sonata that worked ideally on Stein's pianos? It would make for a very neat argument indeed if this particular sonata included a section of unusual texture, or some other 'ideal' reason for using the sustaining levers (the only sort of knee levers on Stein's pianos at the time). Yet it is very difficult to find appropriate moments to use the levers in this sonata – as long as one assumes a technique no more developed than that demonstrated in the earlier pedal markings of the 1790s and other eighteenth-century literature. It is just conceivable that the low As of the fourth variation in the last movement might be sustained by the left lever (Ex. 45); but the left-hand arpeggios are rather low in register and would sound unpleasant if the lever were held for

more than a few beats, and the example is less than convincing in a number
of other ways. Similarly, in variation 6 it would be possible to use the lever to
sustain some of the left-hand octaves which cannot be held for long because of
the hand crossing; but the use of the lever for one or two beats at a time does
not accord with the contemporary descriptions of technique. In the slow movement, where some opportunities might be expected, the harmony simply
moves too quickly for the lever to be effective.

So what did Mozart have in mind? The letter mentions that he performed
this and the other sonatas from memory. Does this mean that he reproduced
them note for note, or did he make changes as he went? Did he, for example,
improvise another variation in the last movement which would have been
ideally suited to the sustaining lever? It is impossible to know. Are we, in any
case, correct in assuming that it was the D major sonata in which the sustaining lever was used? This is far more certain. Mozart also mentions specifically
the sonata in G major. In the last movement of this piece there is an opportunity to introduce the sustaining levers shortly after the repeat signs, for some
dramatic arpeggios lasting for two or four bars. But even this seems a little
out of character, introducing a new tone-quality in the middle of a movement
just for a few bars which are no more significant than any other moment in
the piece.

Perhaps we should not expect to find any obvious places for the use of the
sustaining lever in these pieces. Mozart, after all, wrote these sonatas prior to
his encounter with Stein's piano; moreover he occasionally played some of them
on the clavichord, according to a letter of his dating from just six days after
his visit to Stein. We might therefore expect to find more striking material in
works written subsequent to the visit. In this regard the Sonata in D major
K311 is particularly interesting. It is difficult to date it precisely, but it has
been assumed to have been written in Mannheim, where Mozart stayed at the
end of 1777, shortly after leaving Augsburg. The slow movement of this sonata
has the most intriguing notation at the end of the slow movement in both
the autograph and the first edition (Ex. 46). The downward crotchet stems of
the left-hand accompaniment cannot be realised literally without the
sustaining device. Is this evidence of the composer responding to the knee levers
he had used in Augsburg by writing in a different way for the instrument? It is
indeed a most unusual type of texture for this date – in the works of other
composers left-hand accompanying figures which exceed the span of a ninth
or tenth occur very seldom before the 1790s, when they are often accompanied
by a sign for the sustaining pedal (see Chapter 5). These accompaniments are
quite rare in Mozart's music too. Most significantly, there are no real instances
of this sort of figuration before 1777, although there are passages which hint
in this direction; the fifth variation of K173c (180) and the twelfth variation
of K189a (179). But in these cases the left hand has a figure covering the
interval of a tenth or eleventh with no indication that any notes should be

Ex. 46 W. A. Mozart, Sonata for piano solo in D major K311, second movement, bars 86–93

held for any longer – not even a slur. All this makes the slow movement of the Sonata K311 look even more remarkable and the experience of it seems to have prompted the composer to experiment in similar ways in a few other works such as the Concerto K365 (second movement bars 50ff.) and the Sonata for violin and piano K378 (first movement, bars 1ff.). Almost as intriguing as the Piano Sonata K311 is the Sonata for violin and piano K379, the first movement of which has an extraordinary passage beginning at bar 20 (Ex. 47). Here, much of the left-hand part is written with slurs while the right-hand part begins with an arpeggio written in small notes which looks an ideal texture for the sustaining lever. All of the notes in both hands are part of the same chord, as long as the left-hand slurs last.

None of these passages offers conclusive evidence that Mozart used the sustaining levers, but they are highly suggestive. If he did on these occasions, then his technique would appear to be well in advance of most of his contemporaries, as far as it is possible to tell. It might also suggest that he at

Ex. 47 W. A. Mozart, Sonata for violin and piano in G major K379, first movement, bars 20–3

least considered using the levers in places where the left-hand part had simple harmonic accompaniment but with a smaller interval span, to enrich the tone – as long as the right-hand part did not move too quickly in stepwise motion, or lay above the critical register affected when the left sustaining lever only was used.

If the emergence of this type of left-hand accompaniment in Mozart's music in the late 1770s is intriguing, then its disappearance in the 1780s is equally so. Apart from one or two isolated examples, there is nothing comparable in his music after 1784. This is very odd, especially since this sort of texture was to become so important to pianists a decade later. Perhaps Mozart abandoned it for commercial reasons: at a time when keyboard music might still be played on a harpsichord, this sort of figuration in the middle of a piece might have proved irritating to a performer on that instrument. A more plausible reason, however, concerns the nature of Mozart's instrument, or instruments.

It has been suggested that many of Mozart's early works were played on the harpsichord rather than the piano.[2] This need not detain us here except as a reminder that if it is accepted that many of the early works were written for harpsichord, then it follows that any consideration of pianoforte levers or pedals is irrelevant. For the later works, however, the single most important issue which affects performance is Mozart's purchase of a pedalboard, probably sometime early in 1785.

Mozart's pedalboard

Neither Mozart's own pedalboard, nor any similar instruments survive from the eighteenth century.[3] There are nevertheless several documentary references to it which give us some insight into its use. The earliest of these is a concert announcement:

> On Thursday, 10th March 1785
> Herr Kapellmeister *Mozart*
> will have the honour of giving at the
> I. & R. National Court Theatre
> a Grand Musical Concert
> for his benefit, at which not only a
> *new*, just *finished Forte piano Concerto*
> will be played by him, but also an
> especially *large Forte piano pedale* will
> be used by him in *improvising*. The
> remaining pieces will be announced
> by the large poster on the day itself.[4]

The following day Mozart gave another concert, this time at the Mehlgrube concert hall. The pace of events was almost too much for this father, who complained to his daughter the next day:

If only the concerts were over! It is impossible for me to describe the rush and bustle. Since my arrival your brother's fortepiano has been taken at least a dozen times to the theatre or to some other house. He has had a large fortepiano pedal made, which stands under the instrument and is about two feet longer and extremely heavy. It is taken to the Mehlgrube every Friday and has also been taken to County Zichy's and to Prince Kaunitz's.[5]

Leopold's description of the pedalboard suggests that it was still quite new – new enough for it to be a newsworthy item for Wolfgang's sister, yet already established sufficiently in the Mozart household to have been taken to several concerts. It is not known when Wolfgang played at Prince Kaunitz's, but he gave a concert at Count Zichy's on 21 February.[6] The Mehlgrube concerts which Leopold refers to had been on every Friday since 11 February. Significantly, it was on that date that Wolfgang first performed the Piano Concerto in D minor K466. This piece has puzzled some editors and writers on account of a few apparently unplayable bars near the beginning of the piano's entry (Ex. 48). Example 48 represents a second version of these bars. In the first version, clearly visible in the autograph, there are no chords beneath the right-hand semiquavers, and the bass notes are placed an octave higher,[7] although it appears that the bass notes were changed while the ink was still wet. It is not altogether clear what Mozart played in the first performance; but he played the piece a few days later, on 15 February, and perhaps on other occasions too later in the month, or in March, so it seems likely that the pedalboard was used on one or more of these occasions.

Ex. 48 W. A. Mozart, Concerto for piano in D minor K466, first movement, bars 88–91

A number of important questions arise in connection with Mozart's pedalboard. What was it like? How long did he keep it? What exactly was played on it? In answer to the first of these questions, Leopold's description tells us that it was about two feet longer than the Walter piano and extremely heavy. This strongly suggests a totally independent instrument on top of which sat the Walter piano. This view is supported by the evidence of the piano itself, which shows no signs of any modification: consequently a pull-down mechanism which connected a pedal action to the action of the piano cannot have been used. A pedalboard with independent strings and action must have been expensive – but Mozart was earning well at the time, and could have afforded it.

The exact disposition of the pedalboard is difficult to judge, since no contemporary examples of this type survive. An independent pedal instrument of 1812, by Brodmann, has a range of almost two octaves; but it sits beneath a six-and-a-half-octave piano, so is presumably somewhat larger in compass than Mozart's (whose piano had just five octaves). The rather eccentric kind of short octave (to modern eyes at least) familiar to organists in Salzburg would probably not have been followed because of the difficulty of arranging the strings in the order required within a case that resembled the piano; and we know from Wolfgang's comments about Stein's organs that he was familiar with chromatic pedalboards.[8]

How long did Wolfgang keep the pedalboard? In 1788 he was visited by Joachim Daniel Preisler and Michael Rosing, who both reported private performances on the instrument,[9] as did another writer, Dr Joseph Frank. When an inventory of Mozart's effects was drawn up after his death '1 forte-piano with pedal'[10] was mentioned. Evidently the pedalboard remained in Mozart's possession from 1785 to his death in 1791.

What was played on it? It is tempting to imagine that all of Mozart's music after the spring of 1785 was intended for the pedalboard; but the available evidence will not sustain such a conclusion. To begin with, there is no evidence to suggest that he continued to transport it to concerts: it is quite possible that its weight convinced Mozart that it should remain a domestic instrument! There is also a complete absence of any notes for it in Mozart's music, apart from those already mentioned from the beginning of the D minor Concerto K466. Something of a coherent picture of what he played on the pedal nevertheless emerges from the sources associated with the pedal which are summarised below.

Date	Source	Music played
February 1785	Concerto K466	Concerto
10 March 1785	Concert announcement	Improvisation (+ other items in the concert – the concerto K467?)
12 March 1785	Leopold's letter	at least some of the concert programme
24 August 1788	Preisler and Rosing diaries	Two extemporisations
	Dr Joseph Frank	A fantasia (presumably K475, as it was the only one printed in Mozart's lifetime)

The most common genre in this list is the fantasia – either written down or improvised (assuming that the improvisations were of this type). This is perhaps to be expected, since it is in this sort of piece that different textures can be exploited most easily. It also seems that Mozart used the pedalboard for one or more concertos. K466 has already been discussed, but in addition it is known that K467 was performed in the concert on 10 March. It seems most unlikely that Mozart would have failed to use the pedalboard in this piece as well as for his improvisation. And what about the other concerts mentioned by Leopold? It is likely that these, or other concertos, were played on those occasions.

It is of course impossible to be sure exactly what, or how much, Mozart played with his feet. We can assume, however, that the pedalboard was more than a passing novelty and should at least be considered as appropriate in any of Mozart's keyboard music after the spring of 1785. This has important implications for the use of the knee levers. The first question that needs to be addressed is whether it was possible to use the knee levers at all while the pedalboard was underneath the piano. This seems to have been the case. To judge from the evidence of one of Schmid's instruments[11] and the Brodmann pedalboard already referred to, there are places to rest the foot which allow sufficient pressure to be exerted for the knees to be raised. This of course assumes that the foot is not playing notes on the pedalboard at the time! But even if it was possible for the knee to be raised, in what circumstances would Mozart have wished to do so? We have already seen how he may have used the knee lever to develop new textures in the bass of the instrument; but the pedalboard would surely have made this technique obsolete, an observation which is reinforced by the decline in this type of texture in Mozart's music after 1784. It looks as if the pedalboard curtailed at least some of Mozart's use of the knee levers.

Even if the pedalboard meant a reduction in the use of the knee levers in certain circumstances, however, it cannot be assumed that Mozart stopped using them altogether. Such a conclusion would fail to give sufficient weight to the enthusiasm he expressed over the devices on Stein's pianos (see p. 82 above). It is also clear that the pedalboard could have assisted only in certain types of texture – there are others where the sustaining lever might be much more appropriate. Before any of these are examined in detail, however, we should remind ourselves of some of the principles governing the use of stops, levers and pedals in the early literature and markings.

The mid-eighteenth-century literature makes it clear that tone-modifying devices were regarded as registers: that is, they were employed for sections, or whole movements, in the manner of organ or harpsichord registers. This view is reflected in the number of devices operated by hand stops which would only be employed at points in the music where one hand was not on the keyboard. These registers were sometimes thought of as imitating other instruments, particularly the pantalon. As the century progressed these views persisted, so that many of the earliest markings in the music itself, from the 1790s and 1800s, show evidence of levers or pedals held in position for several bars at a time, or even for whole variations or movements. Evidence for the use of the levers or pedals for less than the duration of a bar is not easy to find in the first instance, but quickly becomes common in the later 1790s; although it may well be that some pianists such as Dussek had experimented in this way at an earlier date, and in a manner similar to that discussed earlier in this chapter. A striking feature of the first pedal markings, when they do eventually appear, is the way in which composers begin to write in new styles to match the new sonorities – extended left-hand figuration, tremolo passages, movements in which the melody is highly triadic, and the harmony scarcely changes, etc.

With these factors in mind, our investigation of suitable places for the use of tone-modifying devices in Mozart's music will concentrate on passages with unusual textures, places where the use of a device would create a particular effect without destroying the continuity of the music, and passages which foreshadow some of the newer textures exploited by pianists in the 1790s. Throughout this investigation it is important to bear in mind the capabilities of the instruments of Mozart's day – the Steins which were so influential, and increasingly common, in southern Germany and Austria, and Mozart's own Walter piano, purchased sometime in the early 1780s. Details of the stops and levers on these instruments were described in Chapter 2.

Ex. 49 W. A. Mozart, Sonata for piano solo in C minor K457, second movement, bars 38–41

Occasionally in Mozart's music a section occurs which uses a texture quite unlike the surrounding passages. If the harmonic movement allows, it may be legitimate to regard such passages as deliberate 'special effects' which can be enhanced by the use of the sustaining lever. Two examples demonstrate this type of writing. The first, bars 38 and 39 from the slow movement of the C minor Sonata K457, occurs after thirty-seven bars of predominantly melodic writing for the right hand above a semiquaver left-hand accompaniment (Ex. 49). For these two bars, however, the 'normal' motion of the movement is suspended, and there are two bars of demisemiquavers, mostly above a pedal G. It is quite unlike anything else in the movement and prepares the listener for a decorated return of the opening theme. The delightful 'haze' that can be created with the sustaining levers (if they are held up for the full two-bar passage) enhances this structurally important moment before the movement returns to the familiar sound of the opening theme. A similar effect can be created at the beginning of the D minor Fantasia K385g, where the harmony moves slowly (the effect is not unlike that called for by Beethoven at the beginning of the C# minor Sonata op. 27 no. 2). In this case, the moderator could be used to enhance the mysterious opening to the piece – there would have been time to release the stop knob on Mozart's piano in the pause after the low A in bar 11, if indeed this piece was written for the Walter. In neither this case nor that of the Sonata K457 could the use of the knee lever (and moderator) be regarded as an intrusion into the music, since the texture is itself so different from the surrounding music. The devices simply enhance an effect already created by Mozart.

A somewhat similar example occurs at the end of the slow movement from the Piano Quartet in E♭ major, where the sustaining levers and perhaps the moderator as well might be used continuously for the last eight bars. The difference between this and the other pieces so far discussed is that the demisemiquavers at the end of the movement are not new – several passages of them have occurred earlier in the piece. Nevertheless their nature and function is different at this point in the movement. The harmony is much slower and less complex, and the whole passage is harmonically inactive, serving as a relaxed end to the coda.

Passages where the sustaining levers might be used for a particular effect without destroying continuity can be found in numerous places. The dramatic arpeggios of concerto cadenzas are particularly appropriate for this sort of use. Example 50, the cadenza from the first movement of K449, is typical, with its sweep over most of the range of the keyboard, and there are many similar examples. The existence of such passages does not necessarily demand the use of the sustaining device, however. Similar arpeggios can be found in the harpsichord repertoire; although it has to be admitted that harpsichord music relies much more heavily on scale patterns, while arpeggios such as those in Example 50 abound at dramatic moments in piano music.

These extravagant gestures are by no means confined to concerto cadenzas. They are particularly common in the fantasias too. It is interesting to spec-

Ex. 50 W. A. Mozart, Concerto for piano in E♭ major K449, first movement cadenza

ulate how Mozart might have played the C minor Fantasia: this piece was entered in his own catalogue on 28 May 1785, a few months after the arrival of his pedalboard. It may be the worked-out, written version of the improvisation that took place with the pedal on 10 March (see above, p. 87). Whether or not this was the case, it was almost certainly the piece that Mozart played on the pedal piano to Dr Joseph Frank (see above, p. 89). How would he have played the dramatic arpeggios in bars 78–83? It is just conceivable that he might have played the lower-octave notes of the left-hand with the left foot while raising the knee levers with his right knee. The overlapping of the knee levers on Mozart's piano would certainly have allowed for this. The sonority produced might almost have been worth the physical contortions involved!

Of the newer styles used by the composers who first marked pedalling in their music there is very little in Mozart's works. We have already seen how he experimented with extended left-hand figurations at the end of the 1770s and beginning of the 1780s – and then apparently discarded this type of writing in favour of sonorities produced with the pedalboard. The tremolo style which was so popular with Steibelt and his contemporaries is almost totally absent from Mozart's works; unless we include in this category variations 10 and 11 from the set based on Baudron's 'Je suis Lindor', composed in 1778. The harmony moves quite quickly in these variations, however, making the sustaining levers less appropriate.

One of the commonest early uses of the sustaining pedal was for slow movements whose harmony and melody moved extremely slowly and unadventurously, according to Louis Adam as well as many early printed examples (see below, p. 171). It is almost impossible to find examples of this in Mozart, however, with the exception of passages such as the end of the slow movement from the E♭ Piano Quartet mentioned above. This point underlines a more fundamental issue relating to the use of knee levers in Mozart – the more general question of style. Any performer who is familiar with good editions of Mozart's music cannot fail to be impressed by the highly ornamental nature of his melodic writing, including as it does all manner of figures in small note values with very specific articulation and dynamic markings – increasingly so with works prepared by Mozart for publication. It is precisely this sort of music that a Stein or Walter piano plays best, as it can express so much fine detail with ease. Any use of the sustaining lever would simply detract from the effect. This sort of writing is not confined to slow movements: many allegro movements carry similarly elaborate indications and the use of the sustaining lever would be most inappropriate.

Finally, very little has been said of the use of the moderator in Mozart's music. There are two reasons for this. First, it is a relatively cumbersome mechanism to use on Mozart's Walter, with its single stop knob in the centre of the nameboard (it does not occur at all as a normal feature on early Steins). Secondly, it alters the sound quality of the instrument so much that its use is always highly noticeable. One or two suggestions have already been made for its use, but it is unlikely that Mozart used it to any great extent.

J. C. Bach

The discussion of the use of stops and levers in Mozart's music underlines the need for detailed information about a particular composer's keyboard instruments before making decisions. This is no less true in the music of other eighteenth-century composers. J C. Bach's op. 5 sonatas, for example, contain a number of places where an ill-informed pianist might assume the use the pedal. The beginning of the development section in the first movement

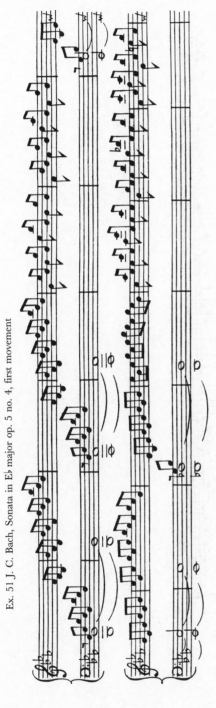

Ex. 51 J. C. Bach, Sonata in E♭ major op. 5 no. 4, first movement

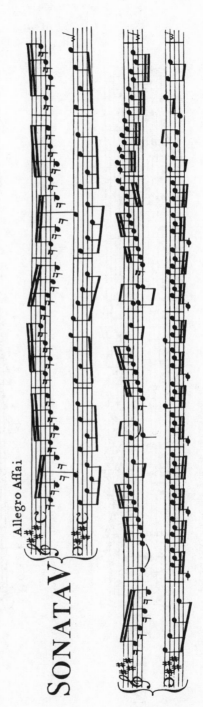

Ex. 52 J. C. Bach, Sonata in E major op. 5 no. 5, first movement

Ex. 53 J. C. Bach, Sonata in C minor op. 5 no. 6, first movement

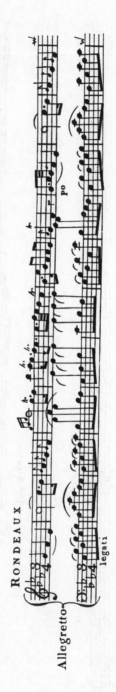

Ex. 54 J. C. Bach, Sonata in E♭ major op. 5 no. 4, final movement

of no. 4 has some impressive broken-chord passages (Ex. 51) and the beginning of no. 5 has some figuration that might similarly benefit from the use of the sustaining pedal (Ex. 52). Yet these sonatas were written for the early English square piano which had only a hand stop mechanism: in neither example could the hand stop be released easily without assistance, especially since they are operated from within the case of the instrument, a short distance from the keyboard itself. Another passage that appears to contain an ideal texture for the sustaining pedal is the beginning of op. 5 no 6 (Ex. 53); but it is possibly an earlier work, from Bach's Italian years,[12] and may well have been written for the harpsichord. Alternatively, it is just conceivable that this is evidence of Bach experimenting on early Italian pianos, although the complete absence of dynamic markings in this sonata (as opposed to several in most of the others) suggests otherwise. Did J. C. Bach intend the use of the stops anywhere in his op. 5 sonatas? It is impossible to answer this with any certainty, but perhaps this is what he had in mind in the final Allegretto of no. 4 (Ex. 54). In addition to slurs over much of the left-hand accompaniment the direction 'legati' occurs – the only time that this term is used in this set. Would Bach have wished this to be played in the same manner as Mme Brillon's performance a few years later in Paris (see p. 32 above)? Bach had sent her a piano but may not have approved the use to which it was put – Dr Burney certainly did not! Elsewhere in Bach's op. 5 set it would be possible to use the sustaining levers for some of the slower movements, particularly those which do not have precise articulation markings.

It can be assumed that much of J. C. Bach's later keyboard music was written for the English grand which Backers had started to make around 1770. Passages such as the four full bars of E♭ major arpeggios in the last movement of the E♭ flat Concerto (c.1772) would sound effective with the sustaining pedal, as might some other similar moments in the concertos (Ex. 55). A

Ex. 55 J. C. Bach, Concerto in E♭ major (c.1772), last movement

particularly strategic arpeggio occurs just before the recapitulation in the first movement of the G major Piano Quartet (Ex. 56) which is effective when played in this way – and rather dull when not. These examples are not found very frequently in J. C. Bach's music, however, and in general his keyboard

Ex. 56 J. C. Bach, Quartet for piano and strings in G major, first movement, bars 123–9

textures are less adventurous than those of the inheritor of his style, Mozart. It is therefore difficult to imagine that Bach had very much use for hand stops or pedals.

C. P. E. Bach

J. C. Bach's older brother Carl Philipp Emanuel evidently approved of the use of the sustaining stop, lever or pedal since he referred to the 'undamped register' of the piano as the 'most delightful' for improvisation.[13] We can assume therefore that it may be used for large sections of at least some of his fantasias – large sections, because he almost certainly had in mind a hand-stop-operated device at the time his comments were made. We can perhaps also assume that it would be less appropriate to use the device in works of a less free nature since the harmonic movement is likely to be quicker and the potential for blurring of the sound much greater. Nevertheless, we should be wary of drawing too many conclusions from our own personal tastes. A some-what curious comment from Sainsbury's dictionary suggests that eighteenth-century taste might have been able to cope with a good deal of music in C. P. E. Bach's style played without the dampers. Speaking of Noelli, one of the last exponents of the pantalon, Sainsbury remarks:

he was intimately acquainted with Emmanuel Bach, and some of his compositions are said much to resemble the style of that great master.[14]

C. P. E. Bach's career spanned several decades during which he experienced some of the most up-to-date piano making, especially in Berlin (see Chapter 1). Nevertheless, we should not expect him or have begun to write in any idiosyncratic ways for the sustaining device, since he was apparently happy to perform on whatever instrument was available, whether it was a harpsichord, clavichord or piano (see p. 12). Only in the very latest sonatas is there evidence that the piano was his preferred instrument. Yet even here there are few, if any, textural innovations. It is perhaps possible to detect an increased use of broken-chord figurations, which might suggest the use of the sustaining device in certain circumstances, but very little music, if any, appears to demand the use of the device.

Haydn

Haydn is another composer whose career spanned several decades. It is unlikely that he encountered the piano early in his life: for much of the time he lived well away from any of the centres where the piano is known to have flour-ished in the middle of the eighteenth century. Indeed, there is no clear evidence that Haydn had anything to do with pianos until the early 1780s – the earliest reference to one at the Esterházy court is in 1781. Modern editors would do well to take note of this, especially in the light of some rather extraordinary assumptions that have been made in the past. One concerns some very unusual writing in the Capriccio Hob.XV11/1, the Variations Hob.XV11/2 and the Sonata Hob.XVI/47. The first of these works is dated 1765 and the other two are presumed to be from the same time. The strange textures are at their most extreme in the Variations (Exx. 57 and 58), where the left-hand part is clearly unplayable as it stands. Some have suggested that the sustaining device is the obvious solution here. If the notes of the intervals or chords are spread, the lower notes can be held with the pedal. This might just be a

Ex. 57 J. Haydn, Variations Hob.XVII/2, Variation 9

Ex. 58 J. Hadyn, Variations Hob.XVII/2, Variation 20

possibility when the pieces are played on a modern piano, although the chord spacing is awkward. It is, however, unlikely that these works were ever intended for the piano: there are no dynamic markings in them and they predate Haydn's known association with the piano by fifteen years. Even if they were for piano, it is unlikely that the instrument would have had any mechanism more sophisticated than hand stops at this date.

There are two other explanations for these passages. The first is that Haydn was writing for a short octave. The problem with this solution is that it assumes either the use of an unusual two-manual instrument or a short octave arrangement that has hitherto not been found on any existing keyboard.[15] This solution is highly complex, but not altogether impossible. A second solution involves the use of a pedalboard. This might make more sense so far as the textures themselves are concerned; but there is no other evidence to suggest that Haydn ever used such a device, so this solution is not without its problems either.

Until more evidence comes to light, the problem of these early Haydn keyboard pieces will remain unsolved. It seems most unlikely that the sustaining lever or pedal is the solution, however, so they need detain us no longer.

Another problem associated with Haydn's keyboard music relates to a much later piece. This is the Sonata in C major Hob.XVI/50 which includes two markings for the 'open pedal' – the only two markings for any such device in Haydn's keyboard music. The work was composed in London in 1794 or 1795, but not published until a few years later. It has been suggested that these 'open pedal' markings are indications for the una corda pedal of English grands.[16] This suggestion can be quickly dismissed, since any familiarity with the English literature of the piano shows that 'open pedal' was in fact the usual term for the sustaining pedal, and that the term was widely used in the music of the period. Latour, for example, while by no means the earliest writer to mention it, nevertheless does so in a succinct manner:

The right hand pedal which is called the Open Pedal, serves to raise the dampers from the strings . . .[17]

What is interesting about the second of Haydn's two markings is its similarity to certain passages in Clementi's piano music. The similarity is all the more intriguing since Haydn's sonata was dedicated to Therese Jansen, a gifted pupil of Clementi. Did Haydn include the passage as a tribute to the most influential pianist in London?

In many instances the material of this chapter raises more questions than it answers. Yet this in the very nature of the subject: it is seldom possible to arrive at 'correct' solutions. What this and earlier chapters set out to achieve, however, is to establish certain guidelines for the appropriate use of tone-modifying devices. The evidence of this chapter in particular demonstrates how important it is to examine the circumstances of each individual composer of the eighteenth century before drawing any conclusions. Ultimately, it is the performer's responsibility to decide whether to use a device.

Pedalling after c.1800

7

The emergence of modern pedalling

Keyboard tutors after Milchmeyer (1797) often contained chapters on pedalling, but for information concerning the first half of the nineteenth century the student has to look well beyond instruction manuals to form a picture of contemporary technique. A more detailed account of pedalling occurred in Louis Köhler's *Systematische Lehrmethode* of 1857–8, but it was Hans Schmitt who produced the first tutor wholly devoted to the subject. *Das Pedal des Claviers* (Vienna 1875) was the published version of four lectures originally delivered to the Vienna Conservatory of Music. It proved to be very influential, passing through at least three German editions. It was quickly acknowledged outside Germany too. Niecks reviewed it enthusiastically in the *Monthly Musical Record* of 1876 and concluded:

And now I'll take leave of the reader with the wish that these remarks may induce those who know German to get and read Herr Schmitt's book, some philanthropist to translate it into English, all to reconsider their use of the pedal. (p. 183)

Niecks' wish for a translation was not fulfilled until 1893, when one appeared in Philadelphia.[1] In the meantime, Köhler was not to be outdone, and in 1882 he published his own tutor wholly devoted to pedalling.[2] Several by other authors followed in both English and German, none of them adding significantly to the technique outlined by Schmitt and Köhler.[3] Some were written from a more practical point of view, such as Rubinstein's, which was published in German in 1896 and appeared in English translation the following year. But even Rubinstein felt compelled to acknowledge his debt to his German predecessors in the preface of his volume:

An explanation of such principles is only found in two works, i.e. those of H. Schmitt and L. Köhler.[4]

In France, a lighthearted pamphlet on the subject of pedalling was published the same year in which Schmitt's book had appeared in Germany[5], but the first major work on the subject was Lavignac's *L'Ecole de la pédale* of 1889. Its description of pedalling techniques is very similar to Schmitt's but it is of additional interest because of its eyewitness accounts of Liszt's and Thalberg's playing. These descriptions show very clearly that the technique which had been so carefully described in these later nineteenth-century writings had their origins in the Liszt–Chopin–Thalberg era – significantly at about the same time that the piano itself was nearing the climax of its development.

Meanwhile, an increasing emphasis on the pedals had been expressed in the earlier nineteenth-century literature. Around 1830, for example, Moscheles observed:

All effects now it seems must be produced by the feet – what is the good of people having hands?[6]

Somewhat later, Friedrich Wieck was less restrained in his criticism:

Cruel fate that invented the pedal! I mean the pedal which raises the dampers of the piano. A grand acquisition, indeed, for modern times! Good heavens! Our piano performers must have lost their sense of hearing! What is all this growling and buzzing? Alas, it is only the groaning of the wretched piano-forte, upon which one of the modern *virtuosos*, with a heavy beard and long hanging locks, whose hearing has deserted him, is blustering away on a bravoura piece, with the pedal incessantly raised, – with inward satisfaction and vain self-assertion! Truly time brings into use a great deal that is far from beautiful: does, then, this raging piano revolutionist think it beautiful to bring the pedal into use at every bar? Unhappy delusion.[7]

During the second quarter of the century Paris was the pianist's capital of Europe and it was there that many innovations took place, as they had done earlier in the century. As before it was the Germans who objected most to these developments, none more so than Wieck:

But who is the frantic musician who is venting his rage on this piano? It is a Parisian or other travelling composer, lately arrived with letters of recommendation, who has just been giving a little rehearsal of what we may expect to hear shortly in a concert at the 'Hôtel de Schmerz'.[8]

These new developments were not welcome even to some ears in Paris, if Hallé is to be believed. In 1840 he inadvertently began a performance of Beethoven's B♭ trio in that city with the pedals disconnected:

The consequence of this untoward accident was that all the critics praised me for my judicious and sparing use of the loud pedal, and this reputation clung to me in Paris ever afterwards, although undeservedly so.[9]

This was a performance of Beethoven's music, however, in which restraint was probably considered appropriate: it is doubtful whether the critics would have spoken so enthusiastically about a performance of Liszt's or Thalberg's music without any pedal!

Such excesses as Wieck describes were fashionable for some time in the middle of the nineteenth century; but by about 1860 some of the wildest enthusiasm for the pedals (as well as other aspects of performance) had abated:

In general it may be said of the pedal, that it is at present – and rightly – more sparingly employed that at the time of Thalbergianism, when entire compositions depended thereon for their effect.[10]

Karl Tausig (1841–1871), later so balanced and superb a person, was at that time, in his youth, still given to wild pounding of the keys and played almost everything with the pedal down.[11]

When, exactly, did this era of 'pedal mania' begin, and who were the pianists responsible? Various nineteenth-century writers attempted classification of pianists according to the style of playing, of which pedalling was an extremely important part. Writing of the sustaining pedal Czerny commented in 1838:

Almost all modern composers employ it often, as Ries, Kalkbrenner, Field, Herz, Moscheles (in his latter works) &c; and it is self evident that the Player must use it whenever he finds it indicated. In Hummel's Works it but seldom occurs, and it may generally be dispensed with.[12]

Later in the same volume Czerny identifies a school of playing more advanced than that of the composers just mentioned:

a. Clementi's style . . .
b. Cramer and Dussek's style . . .
c. Mozart's school . . .
d. Beethoven's style . . .
e. The modern brilliant school founded by Hummel, Kalkbrenner and Moscheles . . .
f. Out of these schools, a new style is just now beginning to be developed, which may be called a mixture of and improvement on all those which preceded it. It is chiefly represented by Thalberg, Chopin, Liszt and other young artists.[13]

Czerny does not specifically mention the pedals in these comments on the school of Thalberg, Chopin and Liszt; but other contemporary writers make it clear that this was an important part of their style which marked them out from earlier pianists:

The smooth, equal and polished styles of Clementi and Cramer, are remarkable for great mechanical correctness and graceful facility. In their schools, all is beautiful, pure, and regular. They admit no such artificial modes of producing tone, as may be observed in the school of Hummel, and still more in that of Moscheles. The latter has several different modes of attacking the keys, according to the effect he wishes to produce; and it is universally allowed that he does not resort in vain to the use of these ingenious contrivances of art peculiar to himself, his style being alike remarkable for variety and brilliancy. There are also peculiar contrivances, though of another kind, in the performance of Liszt, whose school is the most complete deviation from that of Hummel that can well be imagined. Delicacy of touch is by no means the chief object of this master, whose ideas are directed to increasing the powers of the piano, and to the necessity of making it, as much as possible, resemble the effects of an orchestra. Hence those peculiar combinations produced by the frequent employment of the pedals, united to various peculiar modes of striking the keys.[14]

Only Liszt is mentioned here; but other writers make it clear that he was not the sole representative of this more advanced school:

In one distinctive point of technic have players, not distinctively Romantic, gone beyond Clementi's practice or suggestion, viz, the use of the damper pedal. Beethoven used it considerably, and Moscheles (1784–1870) still more extensively. Henselt (born 1814) still further enlarged the domain of the pedal, and Thalberg (1812–1871), who cannot be classed as either a classicist or romanticist, but is the culmination of the 'Philistine' school of shallow players, of which Czerny and Kalkbrenner were distinguished, carried the use of it to its limits.[15]

Finally, Niecks summed it up well when he wrote:

It was not until the time of Liszt, Thalberg and Chopin that the pedals became a power in pianoforte playing.[16]

Pedalling in the nineteenth century evidently went through several phases. To begin with, pianists such as Dussek and Beethoven established the use of the pedals as fundamental to performance on the instrument. Their technique was extended by the next generation, including Kalkbrenner, Moscheles and their contemporaries. Of these, Hummel created for himself a reputation for using the pedals very sparingly, although this view may be more a result of the extremely cautious remarks in his piano tutor than his actual practice. A modern technique appears to have been established in the era represented by Chopin, Liszt and Thalberg, during which time certain excesses in performance were fashionable. The technique developed by these pianists found its way into instruction manuals wholly devoted to the subject, notably that by Hans Schmitt published in 1875. By this time, some of the worst excesses in performance had disappeared in favour of greater refinement.

What, exactly, were the techniques developed by these pianists and what evidence is there of the manner in which individuals used the pedals? Pedal markings in the music itself at first sight appear to tell us all we need to know; but they are not without their difficulties, as Niecks observed:

The differences of opinion with regard to the use of the pedal are indeed of the widest. How little men of ability agree will be seen from the following remarks:–
     Wieck, the well-known teacher, and father of Madame Schumann, writes in a little book on pianoforte-playing and singing, 'Chopin this gifted, tasteful, delicately discriminating composer and virtuoso may serve you as a model in the use of the pedal. If you investigate and observe his careful and delicate notation in his compositions, you will be able to instruct yourselves fully about the right and beautiful use of the pedal.' Now hear Rubinstein, 'Rubinstein reminded me particularly,' says Herr Schmitt, in his book, 'that I should not forget to mention that most of the pedal marks in Chopin's works are wrongly placed.' Again, Weitzmann, in his history of pianoforte-playing, says that Moscheles obtained through the frequent and methodised use of the pedal, which was despised by Hummel, and through the greater power and variety of touch, effects which were unknown to the last-named master, who had

much affinity with him. But in reading Herr Schmitt's lectures we come on the following passage: 'If I forgive Moscheles, whom I otherwise highly revere, the many sins of his notation of the pedal in Hallberger's edition, I do so chiefly because I have found that he does not treat his own works better.' He adds, however: 'But that a finished artist like Moscheles should have used the pedal as he marked it, surely cannot be maintained.'[17]

A possible explanation for these comments lies in the fact that pianists such as Schmitt and Rubinstein were playing on more resonant pianos than those available to either Chopin or Moscheles; hence pedal effects needed to be reconsidered. A more likely reason for the debate, however, lies in the notation itself. Schmitt, and others of his generation, were struggling to find ways of notating the pedals in more precise ways: even a cursory reading of his and Lavignac's pedalling tutors, for example, reveals that they were developing methods of notating whether the pedals were depressed just before, on, or after the beat. Such refinements cannot possibly be indicated with any accuracy by a notation which used the abbreviation 'ped' for the depression of the sustaining pedal. Is the pedal to be depressed at the beginning of the 'p', in the middle of the term, or in some other place? It is impossible to tell and neither composers nor engravers generally took too much trouble over the precise placing of the term (although occasionally a degree of consistency occurs, as we shall see in the next chapter). One reason for this is that the addition of pedal markings usually occurred in the final stages of composition (if at all), and as a result were not infrequently misplaced slightly, to avoid collision with the stem of a note, or some other symbol. In defence of composers such as Chopin and Moscheles it should be added that they were writing at a time when the precise use of the pedals appears to have been discussed very little. The fact that there are a great many pedalling indications in Chopin's music would therefore have been quite satisfactory for Wieck (according to his comments quoted above), especially in view of the notation of his son-in-law, Robert Schumann, who frequently marked at the beginning of a piece only that the pedal should be used, with no further indications of precisely where this should be done.

The nature of the evidence makes it difficult to assess with precision the pedalling techniques of pianists from the first half of the nineteenth century. The didactic literature is generally vague and indications in the music are scarcely more helpful. Pieced together, however, these fragments of information reveal a general picture which demonstrates how pianists developed a sophisticated technique of the sustaining pedal and of the other devices which appeared at various stages of the piano's history. It is these developments which form the substance of the final chapters of this book.

8

The sustaining pedal after c.1800

Chapter 5 showed how some pianists began to use the sustaining pedal to enhance the sonority of the piano in the closing years of the eighteenth century, not just in the higher, weaker register, but also in the middle of the instrument (see Exx. 26 and 27). This represented a change in emphasis from the effect-oriented pedalling of most eighteenth-century sources, as pianists searched for a 'singing' tone on the increasingly resonant piano.

A result of this search for richer sonorities was that pianists began to depress the sustaining pedal for a large proportion of the music. This 'constant' pedalling in turn drew attention to details of technique: how, exactly, was the pedal to be raised and depressed again at each change of harmony – especially in music where the harmonic and melodic writing was becoming more chromatic? The most important answer to this question was syncopated pedalling; the technique whereby the pedal is raised at the moment a chord or note is played, or very shortly afterwards, and depressed again immediately. It is a fundamentally different technique from that in which the pedal is depressed at the same time as the notes, as it enables the performer to produce a seamless legato, even in passages where full chords in both hands mean that all the fingers have to be taken off the notes prior to the next chord being struck.

Three refinements of syncopated pedalling appeared. Two of these have been called 'half pedalling' in some of the literature relating to pedalling, but they are in fact different. In the first of these the pedal is released and then depressed again very quickly in order to damp some of the sound of the strings, but not all. It is particularly useful in passages where a bass note is sustained underneath changing harmony in higher registers which needs to be damped. More time is required to stop the vibration of the larger bass strings than those in the treble, so that a short release of the pedal will damp the higher notes while leaving those in the bass to vibrate, albeit with decreased intensity. The second 'half pedalling' technique simply involves a partial depression of the pedal so that some of the damper felt comes into contact with the string. It is a difficult technique to control, and varies from one instrument to another to such an extent that it has been dismissed by many as too unreliable to be practical. The third technique, tremolo pedalling, is an extension of the first and can be used with particular effect in scale passages, where the foot 'trills' the pedal in order to damp some of the sound while giving the effect of constant pedal. Elements of any one of these three techniques may be found in another. In releasing the pedal and retaking it very quickly, for example (the first technique described above) not all of the felt will necessarily come into contact with the strings (the second technique). It is therefore unnecessary to draw too rigid a distinction between them. All these techniques, and combinations of them, were discussed in pedalling tutors towards the end of the nineteenth century but had in fact developed earlier. To trace these developments precisely is impossible; but a general picture of increasing sophistication in pedalling techniques does emerge in various sources from the earliest years of the century onwards.

Early evidence for syncopated pedalling

In Chapter 5 members of the London school were identified as variously conservative or progressive in their pedalling. Unfortunately, the more progressive members of the school such as Dussek were far from conscientious in marking pedalling in their music. Ironically, it was Clementi, also a publisher, and probably the most conservative member of the school, who provided the most detailed markings in his later music. His music uses textures which rely on the sustaining pedal much less than his contemporaries, but in some of his detailed markings it is nevertheless possible to detect an increasing sophistication in technique coupled with a desire to notate the movements of the foot more carefully. Example 59 is from the beginning of his Fantasia op. 48 published in 1821. In bars 2 and 3 of this example the pedal release sign * is consistently placed on the beat with a precision that suggests more than a mere accident of printing – the delay of the release sign from the end of bar 2 to the beginning of the new system in bar 3 is particularly noteworthy. The markings in these two bars strongly suggest syncopated pedalling. Bar 1, however, is curiously inconsistent. Here, in the third beat, the term 'PED' occurs over the chord in the left-hand part, whereas it would be more appropriately placed over the low B♭, which will not be sustained if the passage is rendered literally. It is difficult to believe that Clementi would have performed this part of the example strictly according to the notation.

This is one example of many in Clementi's late works. Whilst it is not without its difficulties, there is sufficient consistency in these markings to suggest that Clementi was by this time giving some attention to the precise moments at which the pedal should be depressed and released. It also demonstrates that even a conservative like Clementi was no longer content with a legato and tone produced by the fingers alone: bars 2 and 3 of Example 59 could easily be played legato in this way, but the pedal adds a richness to the sound by the sympathetic vibration of the other strings. It is clear evidence that Clementi was beginning to rely on the sustaining pedal for richer sonorities on the instrument.

Ex. 59 M. Clementi, Fantasia op. 48, p. 3

If Clementi, the senior member of the London school, was able to keep abreast of developments in technique, it should not necessarily be assumed that the younger members of the school all did so. Contemporary accounts of Cramer's playing at the end of his life make it difficult to believe that he was using the sustaining pedal very extensively. When Wilhelm von Lenz heard him play in 1842 it was a painful experience. He recorded the following impression after hearing Cramer play some of his studies:

It was dry, wooden, harsh, with no *cantilena* in the third one, in D major. Was *that* Cramer? Had the great man lived so long, only to remain so far behind the times?[1]

Von Lenz does not specifically mention the pedal here, but a lack of it is strongly suggested by his reference to the dryness of Cramer's playing. Hogarth made similar remarks about Cramer and compared him with Hummel, who was well known for his frugal pedalling (see p. 41). By comparison with the accounts of Cramer's late performances, those of Clementi's admittedly rare public appearances are much more complimentary, suggesting that the older man had been more successful in keeping up with the times.[2]

Dussek was the member of the London school most frequently singled out by early nineteenth-century writers as the foremost pianist of his day in the use of the pedals (see p. 38 above). If Clementi was conscious of fine details of pedalling by about 1820, it is likely that Dussek had developed similar techniques by the end of his life (he continued to perform until just before his death in 1812). This was certainly the view of Chaulieu, who wrote about Dussek some years after the latter's death:

The skilful way in which he used the only pedal he chose to adopt, the new effects that he managed, excited general admiration, and the disdain that he manifested towards the others abolished them forever.

To many readers, forgetting that we labour for the young, who generally ignore what happened twenty years ago, we say: why this long preamble?

The preamble was necessary for understanding that which will follow: because following the various revolutions experienced by the pedals, that of the dampers at last reigns alone today.

Now, how Dussek used it; that was at first a mystery; and while some said that he never left it, others claimed, with some reason, that he made it move like the handle of a knife-grinder.

Indeed, he used it in this manner:- the foot always placed on the lever, an elastic pressure, so to speak, permitted him to make the strings vibrate all the more strongly. Yet he had his leg still, and could therefore infinitely vary the pressure on the pedal.[3]

Chaulieu was a pupil at the Conservatoire at the beginning of the century and became an important figure in the musical life of Paris during the first quarter of the century. He would have had opportunity to hear the most influential pianists of his day in Paris. It is therefore all the more remarkable that he singled out Dussek, who had been dead for over twenty years at the time Chaulieu was writing, as his model for pedalling.

Chaulieu's description of Dussek's pedalling suggests that the latter held the sustaining pedal down a great deal of the time ('some said that he never left it'). Another pianist, Friedrich Kalkbrenner, who was a young man during Dussek's last years in Paris, made the same observation:

Dussek, in particular, was remarkable . . . for he kept the mufflers almost constantly lifted when he played in public.[4]

In order to do this without unduly blurring the sound his technique resembled 'the handle of a knife-grinder', according to Chaulieu. It seems that Dussek in some way created the effect of constant pedal while continually clearing the sound by releasing it, and depressing it again immediately. A little later in his article Chaulieu described this technique in more detail. He does not specifically attribute it to Dussek, but these later remarks follow so closely on his description of Dussek's playing that it is hard to avoid the conclusion that Dussek used this technique:

Composers in general are not very careful as regards the indication of the pedals, and particularly so when marking its release. There is, moreover, a very important movement of the foot, which could be called Breathing, in comparison with the action of the singer's lungs. This movement is performed by raising and putting down the foot again immediately, in such a manner that the confusion ceases while the action of the pedal appears uninterrupted.

Careful writers, to express this effect, multiply this: Pédale-Otez-Pédale-Otez etc. (A). Their music, already overloaded with signs, then becomes encumbered, and often laziness or misplacing forces them to neglect useful details. In these circumstances I use a sign which indicates at the same time the release and immediate retaking of the pedal; in short, a breathing:

If one is convinced of this truth, that it is better not to use the pedal than to use it without discernment, one will recognise the usefulness of the sign I propose. It has the form of an O obliquely crossed by a line. It is sufficient to cast one's eyes on the examples in illustration B to understand its application . . .[5]

Unfortunately, the examples to which Chaulieu refers labelled 'A' and 'B' appear not to have been printed; but a good idea of the effect he intended can be gained from contemporary printed scores of his, one of which is reproduced as Example 60. Whilst Chaulieu nowhere explicitly states that the pedal should be raised on the beat and immediately depressed again, the description he gives of the effect of continuous pedal, with the numerous examples in his music, such as Example 60, make it clear that the desired result could only be achieved with syncopated pedalling. Unfortunately, his new notation was not taken up by others.

Ex. 60 C. Chaulieu, 18 Elegant Studies, no. 7

The evidence is admittedly scant, but there is sufficient at least to suggest that some pianists were aware of sophisticated techniques such as syncopated pedalling soon after the beginning of the nineteenth century. If these pianists were forward-looking, however, others were inevitably much less convinced about the use of the pedals, even in Paris, as Gardeton observed in 1820:

It is rare that the great pianists make use of their help; they generally regard this mechanism as more suitable for producing confusion in the harmony; for introducing variety into the performance . . . Clever masters wish, so to speak, that the pedals are only to be found at the end of their fingertips.[6]

Developments from c.1830

The evidence for more advanced pedalling techniques in the first quarter of the century is thin, but more detailed information begins to emerge from 1830 onwards. Kalkbrenner, for example, discusses an instance where the sustaining pedal may be depressed after the note has been sounded:

The loud pedal may be successfully employed for a single chord, or for many in succession, provided it be relinquished each time the harmony changes; occasionally, taken after a note has been struck, it causes it to revive . . .[7]

Czerny offers what appears to be a description of syncopated pedalling:

In the *Tremolando*, the damper pedal is almost always necessary; but the pedal must always be relinquished and resumed at every change of chord . . . The quitting and resuming the pedal must be managed with the utmost rapidity, not to leave any perceptible chasm or interstice between the chords; and must take place strictly with the first note of each chord.[8]

Thalberg is also specific about the exact moment at which the pedals should be depressed in his *Art du chant* of 1853:

Frequently, for particular effects, they must only be employed after the long melody notes have been struck.[9]

Such moments are not marked in Thalberg's scores, which only contain an outline of the pedalling required, as Zimmerman had noted in 1840:

We must first be content with taking the pedal in those places indicated by the composer; however, some composers (Thalberg for example) indicate it much less than they use it, so as not to multiply signs.[10]

An extremely detailed illustration of what another writer claims to be Thalberg's technique appears in Lavignac's pedalling tutor of 1889. Although this tutor was published long after the event, Lavignac's comments were based on an eyewitness experience:

The first time that I had the occasion to hear the celebrated Thalberg, one of the kings of the pedal (it was in the old Erard hall, a long time ago), I was placed in the first row of the stalls, that is to say, very near to the piano, almost under the piano. I remember being immensely astonished at first, observing that Thalberg was afraid, that his foot trembled on the pedal to the extent that he could not hold it down for half a second. But this delusion did not last long; it could not have done. The calm style of Thalberg's playing, majestic, sober, imposing, perfectly correct and perhaps a little cold, by no means accorded with the notion of a paralytic emotion. Thalberg was not afraid, but he used the pedal admirably with very brief touches brilliantly distributed just at the required moment and with such frequent repetition that at first, a little naively, I had thought it a trembling. The impressions of youth are so strong that I should not fail to see in this memory, so distant as it may be, the origin of this work, which always seems to have been a project.

Attention once called to the subject, I have never neglected to observe the way in which great pianists use the pedal on every occasion that I have been able to – I have never seen any take it on the beat on purpose, to beat time, but almost always a little before or a little after, depending on the circumstances – All use it, especially in passages containing diatonic or chromatic patterns, and often without releasing it, all use rapid movements of half pedalling that we represent in our graphic system by broken lines ⌐/\/\/\/\/\⌐ . There are those who use these rapid and almost imperceptible movements in such a way that it could be said that not a single note of the piece has been played without the pedal; but in that case the movements are so frequent and so close together that the pedal is renewed on almost every note, in such a manner that could not cause any trouble in the harmony.[11]

Although many of Lavignac's comments concern Thalberg in particular he also heard and observed other pianists, among them Liszt. Lavignac observed:

By spirited and violent effects [and] clear-cut contrasts, he excelled more than anyone in reproducing the inflexions of the human voice with his piano, and he obtained positively the illusion of swelled sounds by taking the pedal *after the note* in long melodic phrases.[12]

As well as the written description of various pianists' playing, Lavignac included in his tutor a specimen of pedalling from a piece by Thalberg. This example, he claims, is how 'Thalberg himself interpreted his markings' (Ex. 61).[13]

By the middle of the nineteenth century, and in the playing of pianists such as Thalberg and Liszt, pedalling had reached a peak of sophistication. We have already seen how this was an era of excess for pedalling, out of which came a more considered period during which the first pedalling tutors emerged (see Chapter 7). But what were the characteristics of individual pianists during this era?

German and Austrian pianists

The conservatism shown by many German and Austrian pianists has already been noted on several occasions. According to the nineteenth-century literature this trend continued well into the middle of the century. Predictably, Hummel proved to be the focus of much critical comment:

Ex. 61 A. Lavignac, *L'Ecole de la pédale*, p. 67

He was an extremist; and in his graceful, clear, elegant, neat, though not grand playing, often lost fine effects, which would have been produced by the correct and judicious use of the pedal.[14]

But Hummel was by no means the only conservative. Czerny also cautioned against over-pedalling:

Many players have so accustomed themselves to employ the same, that a pure and classical performance with the fingers only, has been almost totally neglected – that some are scarcely in a position to perform a simple four-part, connected passage duly *legato* without a pedal . . .[15]

To portray Czerny as uncompromisingly conservative would be mistaken, however. Elsewhere in the same volume he recognised the sustaining pedal's usefulness:

By means of this pedal, a fullness can be attained which the fingers alone are incapable of producing.[16]

His comments imply that he was not wholly in sympathy with the style represented by Dussek, Thalberg and others, in which the dampers were raised for as much of the time as possible, but not averse to using the pedal for a richer tone on occasion.

A later advocate of the finger-legato described by Czerny was Henselt:

Henselt's way at the keyboard may be taken as the link between Hummel's and Liszt's; that is to say, with Hummel's strictly legato touch, quiet hands and strong fingers, Henselt produced effects of rich sonority something like those which Liszt got with the aid of the wrists and pedals.[17]

Accounts of Henselt's playing suggest that he was somewhat obsessive in his finger technique, and spent many hours stretching his fingers with arpeggios. Nevertheless he realised the usefulness of the pedals, even if at times he continued to expend needless effort with his fingers while using it:

Henslet's way of holding the keys down as much as possible with the fingers, over and above keeping the dampers raised by means of the pedals, does not seem the most practical.[18]

Clara Schumann was an important nineteenth-century figure whose technique of the pedal was extremely refined. Her opinion on the subject of pedalling can be deduced from her comments about others:

We have been hearing Liszt . . . He cannot be compared to any other player – he stands alone. He arouses terror and amazement, and is a very attractive person. His appearance at the piano is indescribable – he is an original – he is absorbed by the piano. His passion knows no bounds, not infrequently he jars on one's senses of beauty by tearing melodies to pieces, he used the pedal too much, thus making his works incomprehensible if not to the professionals at least to amateurs.[19]

I found Nicolaus Rubinstein in Moscow – the man has amazing technique, though his fingers are small and thick, but for the most part he plays only drawing-room pieces, thumps in the latest fashion with a great deal of everlasting pedal and no sentiment but that of the soft pedal.[20]

Evidently she was a true child of her father; but it is a pity that her reserve in pedalling matters was not translated into detailed, precautionary markings in her music, which contains only the most general of pedalling indications:

The correct use of the pedals with strict observance of the changes in harmony is the general rule. It is only marked in places where it is obligatory.[21]

Clara Schumann must have been yet another pianist who 'interpreted her own pedal markings', just as Lavignac had observed with Thalberg (see p. 116 above).

  Moscheles' playing was enthusiastically reviewed by Robert Schumann but was apparently considered 'frightfully baroque' by Chopin,[22] presumably on account of his finger technique. Chopin's biographer, Niecks, was rather more charitable, attributing this trait to Moscheles' particular position in the evolution of piano technique. Niecks considered him the first to make

a more extensive and artistic use of the pedals, although also he employed them sparingly compared with his . . . younger contemporaries.[23]

But Moscheles' 'sparing' use of the pedal was probably somewhat antiquated, even by the standards of his contemporaries. A comment in his Studies op. 70, published in 1825 or 1826 suggests that he was slow to adopt syncopated pedalling:

Previous to a change of harmony the Pedal must be carefully taken off, and again used at the beginning of a new one.[24]

If the text is followed precisely, Moscheles' remarks require the pedal to be raised *before* the change of harmony, not *with* it. The pedal markings in the music itself concur with his instructions – the release signs are consistently placed before the end of the beat (Ex. 62). For a pianist of Moscheles' stature to be apparently so far behind the times is surprising. Was he simply unaware of syncopated pedalling, or did he actually prefer the more articulated style that inevitably results from pedalling on the beat (often referred to as 'rhythmic' pedalling)? To what extent was his playing typical of his German contemporaries? The answers to these questions can only be guesses; but even more remarkable than Moscheles' apparent conservatism is the reluctance of some later pianists to adopt syncopated pedalling, to the extent that Matthay wrote in Boston as late as 1913:

I think it must be taken for granted that even the most primitive and antediluvian of teachers have now at least some hazy sort of notion as to the nature and importance of 'syncopated' pedalling.[25]

In London, twenty-four years later still, Edith Hipkins commented:

Ex. 62 I. Moscheles, Studies op. 70, p. 41

Jean Kleczynski states that with Chopin the pedal followed the note, an effect still in some quarters considered a novelty.[26]

Evidently, it was not just German nineteenth-century pianists who were slow to adopt syncopated pedalling: both Matthay and Hipkins suggest that it was not universally accepted until well into the twentieth century.

New textures – three-hand technique

If there were several pianists who were reluctant to adopt more progressive techniques of the sustaining pedal, there were others who revelled in the new textural possibilities which the pedal made available. In the 1790s and 1800s pianists of the French and English schools rapidly adopted extended left-hand accompaniment textures (see above, pp. 57–74). It was not long before whole movements were composed in which this figuration was a principal feature. It was to become a highly prominent element of the 'nocturne style' pioneered by Field and developed by Chopin.[27] Other textures were also developed. Example 63 is taken from a song by Prince Louis Ferdinand (Dussek's pupil), who died in 1806. The vocal melody is doubled in the left-hand part, which also plays an accompanying role in a lower register. This effect would be impossible without the sustaining pedal. It is a technique not dissimilar to one that was to become famous in the middle of the nineteenth century – the

Ex. 63 Prince Louis Ferdinand, 'Die Wolke'

three-hand technique. This was an effect in which a melody was sustained in the middle register of the piano while figurations of all sorts were played to either extremity of the piano, the whole effect relying heavily on the sustaining pedal (see Ex. 61). Czerny was fascinated by it and various aspects of the technique occupy most of the first chapter of the Supplement to his piano tutor.[28] It is a texture often associated with Thalberg, who used it extensively in operatic fantasias:

As distinguished from any other pianist of the time, his speciality was the surrounding of a melody with arabesques and ornamented passages of scales and arpeggios played with rapidity, clearness, and brilliancy.[29]

Moscheles (Thalberg's teacher) wrote:

His theme, which lies in the middle part, is brought out clearly in relief with an accompaniment of complicated arpeggios which remind me of a harp. The audience is amazed.[30]

But while Thalberg's reputation as a pianist was greatly enhanced as a result of using the technique, he was not the inventor of it:

Pollini indeed may, in this respect, be considered as an inventor, having anticipated Thalberg in the extended grasp of the keyboard by the use of three staves . . . thus enabling the player to sustain a prominent melody in the middle region of the instrument, while each hand is also employed with elaborate passages above and beneath it. This remarkable mode of producing by two hands almost the effect of four [!], appears indeed to have been originated by Pollini in his 'Uno de trentadue Esercizi in forma di toccata', brought out in 1820.[31]

Nevertheless the effect became associated with Thalberg, who popularised it at a time when 'pedal mania' was reaching its height.

Liszt and Thalberg

During this period, as we have already seen, a thoroughly modern and sophisticated pedalling technique was developed by three pianists in particular – Thalberg, Liszt and Chopin. They were renowned for their pedalling, yet from contemporary accounts of their playing it is clear that there were significant differences in their performance styles: as Niecks noted, 'every pianist of note has, of course, his own style of pedalling'.[32] These individual styles arose from the particular aims of pianists, and the circumstances of performance. In the case of Thalberg and Liszt, the circumstances were identical – both frequently played in concert halls to large audiences, as well as in more intimate settings – but their overall aims could not have been more different. Thalberg was a controlled, refined, perfect virtuoso with an excellent technique and exquisite taste. Liszt possessed an equally fine technique, but his performances were noted for their unpredictable, demoniac qualities that held audiences spellbound:

Liszt's attitude at the piano, like that of a pythoness, has been remarked again and again. Constantly tossing back his long hair, his lips quivering, his nostrils palpitating, he swept the auditorium with the glance of a smiling master..

Thalberg was the gentlemen artist, a perfect union of talent and propriety. He seemed to have taken it for his rule to be the exact opposite of his rival. He entered noiselessly: I might almost say without displacing the air. After a dignified greeting that seemed a trifle cold in manner, he seated himself at the piano as though upon an ordinary chair. The piece began, not a gesture, not a change of countenance! not a glance towards an audience! If the applause was enthusiastic, a respectful inclination of the head was his only response. His emotion, which was very profound, as I have had more than one proof, betrayed itself only by a violent rush of blood to the head, colouring his ears, his face and his neck. Liszt seemed seized with inspiration from the beginning; with the first note he gave himself up to his talent without reserve, as prodigals throw their money from the window without counting it, and however long was the piece his inspired fervour never flagged.

Thalberg began slowly, quietly, calmly, but with a calm that thrilled. Under those notes so seemingly tranquil one felt the coming storm. Little by little the movement quickened, the expression became more accentuated, and by a series of gradual crescendos he held one breathless until a final explosion swept the audience with an emotion indescribable.

I had the rare good fortune to hear these two great artists on the same day, in the same salon, at an interval of a quarter of an hour, at a concert given by the Princess Belgiojoso. There was then revealed to me palpably, clearly, the characteristic difference in their talent. Liszt was incontestably the more artistic, the more vibrant, the more electric. He had tones of a delicacy that made one think of the almost inaudible tinkling of tiny spangles or the faint explosion of sparks of fire. Never have fingers bounded so lightly over the piano. But at the same time his nervosity caused him to produce sometimes effects a trifle hard, a trifle harsh . . .

At this concert, in hearing Liszt I felt myself in an atmosphere charged with electricity and quivering with lightning. In hearing Thalberg I seemed to be floating in a sea of purest light. The contrast between their characters was not less than between their talent.[33]

In the light of such descriptions it comes as no surprise to learn that Thalberg's pedalling technique was extremely refined, allowing for no harsh effects or confusion of sound:

His use of the pedal was as good as a lesson to any student of the piano.[34]

Thalberg, famous master and model virtuoso, employed the pedals with a wonderful touch. Following his example, pianists of the French school are also distinguished by the use that they made of this method.[35]

Like Chopin, Thalberg constantly used the soft and loud pedals in an alternating or simultaneous manner, but with so perfect a touch that the most sensitive ear could not perceive any abnormal resonance.[36]

The legato story is true – few possess the art. Joseffy achieved the legato effect by an aerial handling – or footing – of pedals. But the clinging legatissimo of Pachmann, Thalberg and Paderewski (in his prime) he did not boast.[37]

In comparison, Liszt's technique was less delicate:

Liszt, who has already rid himself of numerous faults, still has one bad habit to lose, that of stamping with his foot when using the pedal, and marking the time by the same means.[38]

Clara Schumann's objections to it have already been recorded (p. 118 above). Sometimes Liszt required very grand pedal effects. Amy Fay described an occasion when he held the pedal down for a lengthy passage:

It was a long arpeggio, and the effect he made was, as I had supposed a pedal effect. He kept the pedal down throughout and played the beginning of the passage in a grand *rolling* sort of manner, and then all the rest of it with a very pianissimo touch, and so lightly, that the continuity of the arpeggio was destroyed, and the notes seemed to be just *strewn* in . . .[39]

Yet one should be wary of drawing the conclusion that Liszt always pedalled more heavily and boldly than Thalberg. Liszt had the ability to play in a number of styles, as the occasion demanded, and while some commentators were impressed by an almost reckless quality, others noted his clarity:

One of the transcendent merits of his playing was the crystal-like clearness which never failed for a moment even in the most complicated and, to anybody else, impossible passages.[40]

This comment is all the more remarkable when seen in context: Hallé had just been describing the 'dazzling splendour' with which he 'subjugated' his hearers in the concert hall, and goes on to describe the incomparable power that he drew from the instrument.[41]

In view of these descriptions of Liszt's playing it would be useful to be able to discover in greater detail the extent to which he created blurred effects with the pedal, or treated it in other 'unorthodox' ways. Given the large number of his pupils it might be imagined that at least a few of them would have left some detailed information; but there is surprisingly little. Despite Amy Fay's remark that 'his touch and his peculiar use of the pedal are two secrets of his playing'[42] she later confessed that 'nobody ever said anything to me about the pedal particularly, except to avoid the use of it in runs, and I supposed it was a matter of taste'.[43] Friedheim wrote that 'another pupil complained that Liszt had not taught him to use the pedals properly.'[44] Amy Fay did, however, leave some indication of the nature of Liszt's pedalling, following her study with Ludwig Deppe in 1873:

Among other refinements of his teaching, Deppe asked me if I had ever made any pedal studies. He picked out that simple little study of Cramer's in D major in the first book – you know it well – and asked me to play it. I had played that study to Tausig, Liszt's favourite pupil, and he found no fault with my use of the pedal; so I sat down thinking I could do it right. But I soon found I was mistaken, and that Deppe had very different ideas on the subject. He sat down and played it phrase by phrase, pausing between each measure, to let it 'sing'. I soon saw that it is possible to get as great a virtuosity with the pedal as with anything else, and that one must make a careful study of it. You remember that I wrote to you that one secret of Liszt's effects was his use of the pedal, and how he has a way of disembodying a piece from the piano and seeming to make it float in the air? He makes a spiritual form of it so perfectly visible to your inward eye, that it seems as if you could almost hear it breathe! Deppe seems to have almost the same idea, though he has never heard Liszt play. 'The pedal', said he, 'is the *lungs* of the piano'. He played a few bars of a sonata, and in his whole method of binding the notes together and managing the pedal, I recognised Liszt. The thing floated! Unless Deppe wishes a chord to be very brilliant, he takes the pedal *after* the chord instead of simultaneously with it. This gives it a very ideal sound.[45]

It is extraordinary that such an apparently great teacher as Liszt had neglected to explain something so essential to his style as syncopated pedalling.

Liszt's pedal markings are scarcely more helpful than his pupils. The B minor Sonata, for example, contains no indications for the sustaining pedal in the autograph, which underwent careful revision in many other respects. In the Tannhäuser Overture transcription a single indication appears at the beginning: 'Judicious use of the pedal is the general rule.' Other pieces are somewhat better served, but there is little information of a really detailed nature, even in works where he experimented with signs for refinements of performance such as accelerando, rallentando and a pause of shorter duration than the usual marking.[46] Some interesting and potentially revealing markings do sometimes occur. In the sonata *Après une lecture de Dante* there are indications which suggest some very extreme blurring (Ex. 64). If the sustaining pedal is depressed for as long as indicated, a disagreeable jumble of sound will result. Even if part of the sound is damped by a quick, or partial, release of the pedal at each chord change the effect will still be very blurred. It is difficult to escape the conclusion that Liszt wanted a deliberately intense, even unpleasant sound here.

Chopin

Liszt and Thalberg were pianists who excelled in the concert hall, where grand gestures and daring effects were appropriate. In contrast, Chopin's style was ideally suited to a more intimate environment, where every detail could be heard. Consequently his technique was extremely refined, as a number of descriptions testify:

In the use of the pedal he had likewise attained the greatest mastery, was uncommonly strict regarding the misuse of it, and said repeatedly to the pupil: 'The correct employment of it remains a study for life.[47]

Ex. 64 F Liszt, *Après une Lecture de Dante*, bars 35–43

No pianist before him employed the pedals alternately or simultaneously with so much tact and skill. With most modern virtuosos, excessive, continuous use of the pedal is a capital defect, producing sonorities eventually tiring and irritating to the delicate ear. Chopin, on the contrary, while making constant use of the pedal, obtained ravishing harmonies, melodic whispers that charmed and astonished.[48]

Chopin had penetrated the secret better than any other master. He gave to his pupils several rules which only later found a place in the usual methods.[49]

Perhaps the highest accolade of all came from Liszt, in an account of a visit he paid to Chopin. Chopin had been working on the Nocturne op. 37 no. 2. Liszt wrote:

He thereupon played it to me and entranced me with its beauties, which under his ravishing touch and incomparably artistic use of the pedals, sounded if possible more divinely beautiful than it is possible to describe in words.[50]

Chopin's highly refined technique demanded a similarly refined piano. His preference for Pleyel's instruments has been well-documented.[51] Liszt described 'these Pleyel pianos which he [Chopin] particularly cherished for their silvery and slightly veiled sonority and their lightness of touch', in contrast to the heavier Erards. Marmontel commented on the pedals of Pleyel's pianos:

The timbre produced by the pedals on Pleyel pianos has a perfect sonority, and the dampers work with a precision very useful for chromatic and modulating passages.[52]

With such a subtle technique, and an appropriate instrument on which to use it, we should not expect Chopin to resort to the pedals automatically to create a particular effect. In some circumstances, for example, he might require the fingers alone to provide a clarity that was impossible with the pedal. This is suggested by a number of contemporary accounts, as well as certain markings in his music. One of Chopin's most devoted students, Mikuli, advised: 'use the pedal with the greatest economy'.[53] The account of another pupil, Mme de Courty, suggests that Chopin advised against the pedal in the earlier stages of a piece's preparation:

Chopin did not want me to use the pedal, yet he himself used it, particularly the soft pedal – without however indicating this to his pupils, in order not to exaggerate or overstep its resources.[54]

This is confirmed by a remark made to Debussy by Mme Mauté, who claimed to have studied with Chopin:

I have very precise recollections of what Mme Mauté told me. Chopin wanted his pupils to practise without the pedal, and, except on very rare occasions, to avoid its use altogether.[55]

Kleczynski identified some passages which might be played without pedals:

many passages are best when played simply and without the use of either pedal. This may be said of [the first section of] the Nocturne in F (op. 15/1), and the middle part, in 3/4 time, of the *Andante spianato* (op. 22).[56]

Both passages are marked *semplice*. In addition to these, others could perhaps be added, such as the Prelude in B minor op. 28 no. 6, whose left-hand part would gain in clarity without pedal, apart from bars 13 and 14, the centre of the work, where the texture is at its widest and the left-hand writing less melodic (as well as the end of the piece); or the E minor Prelude op. 28 no. 4 where the natural restraint of the piece could be enhanced with a finger-legato rather than the more clumsy sustaining pedal.

There are certain passages in Chopin's own autographs where the composer has crossed out pedalling, showing how careful he was in some circumstances to avoid any hint of harmonic blurring. The Prelude in E major op. 28 no. 9 for example, has two instances where the pedal release sign has been moved to the left by a whole beat, at the end of bars 1 and 4 (Ex. 65). In bar 1, it may have been an oversight on Chopin's part at first to place the release sign at the end of the bar, causing harmonies of E and A major to overlap. Bar 4 appears to be more significant, however. At first he seems to have envisaged the trill with its four-note termination played with the pedal held down since the beginning of the third beat. There is no change of harmony here (at least, not until the last right-hand chord of the bar), but Chopin evidently required a greater degree of clarity in the left-hand part on the last beat of the bar, so he moved the pedal release sign underneath the trill. On a somewhat larger

Ex. 65 F. Chopin, Prelude in E major op. 28 no. 9

scale, Chopin removed the pedalling from a chord passage at the end of the Ballade in F major op. 38 (bar 198), creating a subtle distinction in sound between this and other chord passages.

Clarity seems to have been of paramount importance to Chopin; but there are occasions on which he appears to have deliberately blurred the pedalling in order to create a particular effect. In the Prelude in B♭ minor op. 28 no. 16 he originally wrote a pedal change on the half bar for the passage that begins in bar 2 (Ex. 66). There is no change of harmony here, but the right hand plays semiquaver scales, so that some damping of the sound seems appropriate. In the event, however, Chopin indicated the pedal to be depressed at the beginning of bar 2 and not raised again until the end of bar 4. Even on an early piano there would still be a significant amount of blurring here. But is this really what Chopin had in mind? In the light of Lavignac's description of the manner in which Thalberg interpreted his own pedal markings it is possible that Chopin did something more sophisticated here. A simple release of the pedal on the half bar would, after all, still leave several adjacent notes resonating together in the right-hand part, albeit for just half a bar rather than three complete bars. It would also interrupt the flow of this phrase, which clearly needs to be performed in a continuous manner. Might Chopin have used some sort of half-pedalling technique throughout these bars? It is highly unlikely that we will ever discover exactly what Chopin did at moments like this; but we should be wary of drawing too many conclusions from a notation that is somewhat imprecise.

Ex. 66 F. Chopin, Prelude in B♭ minor op. 28 no. 16

Chopin was much more forthcoming in his advice to pupils than Liszt. Copies of his works annotated by himself or pupils exist with a number of alterations which suggest that he was keenly aware of the effects of pedalling. In a number of instances missing pedalling has been supplied[57] and in others the printed pedalling has been altered, typically by changing the position of the release sign slightly to avoid blurring as in the Etude op. 25 no. 2 bars 18–19, in which the sign has been brought forward half a bar. On other occasions Chopin was at pains to point out a precise effect. In the Prelude in B minor op. 28 no. 6 a vertical line links the pedal release sign with the fourth quaver of the right-hand part, showing the precise moment at which the pedal should be taken off. Such details of pedalling not only exist in copies of the music; they were noted by contemporaries. Liszt related one such detail regarding the F minor passage beginning at bar 138 of the Polonaise in A♭ major op. 53:

'In this register of the piano, don't just play the basses *sforzando*, that is, reinforced', said Liszt, 'but give them a slightly lingering accentuation, like the muffled rumbling of a distant cannon. The pedal will help to obtain this effect. The idea isn't my own', he added, 'I've often heard Chopin play it like that.'[58]

Later developments

The nineteenth-century documents detailing the developments of pedalling in general and the evidence associated with particular pianists demonstrate that all the fundamental elements of a modern pedalling technique were in existence by the middle of the century. This is not surprising in view of the fact that the piano as we know it today had essentially reached the end of its development by about the same time. The Steinways and Chickerings of the second half of the century may differ somewhat in tonal quality and in some minor details from today's instruments, but they share the same characteristics of prolonged resonance and increased volume brought about by heavier construction and increased string tension. Pedalling problems for the mid-nineteenth-century pianist were therefore very similar to those faced by the present-day performer.

As developments in pedalling slowed, a change of emphasis in the didactic literature began to emerge. Whereas tutors at the end of the nineteenth century had concentrated on exposing the 'secrets' of pedalling in the Chopin–Liszt–Thalberg era, the later literature began to address other problems although it of course continued to be necessary to give at least some space to the details of syncopated pedalling and other elements of technique.

It is clear that important differences continued to exist between various schools of pedalling. Lindo, for example, commented in 1922:

It may not be amiss . . . to call attention to the fact that there exist two schools of pedalling, with divergent and even somewhat antagonistic aims. So little has this subject been studied scientifically and systematically that it is doubtful if the existence of two methods is actually realised even by their respective exponents. The chief points of difference are that according to one method the pedal should – at any rate in the classics – be resorted to mainly in order to add body and colour to chords and chord passages, whilst according to the other it should be called upon to supply a harmonic background to nearly every type of passage.[59]

The issue of 'the classics' had in fact been discussed as early as Adam (see the Appendix pp. 170–73) and Czerny, who noted that in 'Mozart's School . . . The Pedal [is] seldom used, and never obbligato',[60] but nineteenth-century writers tended not to go into detail to the same extent as their twentieth-century counterparts. Busoni, for example, advocated its use in the most discreet manner possible when playing Bach:

in the piano works [of J. S. Bach] the inaudible use of the pedal is the only proper one. By this we mean the employment of the pedal for binding two successive single tones or chords, for emphasizing a suspension, for sustaining a single part, etc.; a manner of treatment by which no specific pedal-effect is brought out.[61]

Busoni shows here a commendable awareness of style and his words are echoed in a number of later writings, many of which are quoted in Riefling's chapter on the subject.[62] More recently, however, another factor has entered the discussion; if stylistic awareness is something to be encouraged, then why not perform Bach's keyboard music on the instrument for which it was most probably intended – the harpsichord? This is not the place for debating that particular point, but it has at least highlighted a slightly different issue for pianists; if Bach's music is to be performed on the modern piano, rather than the harpsichord, then why not use the full resource of the instrument if it makes the performance more effective? Cautious movement in this direction can be found, for example, in Banowetz's chapter on Bach.[63]

Another factor that has concentrated pianists' minds on the use of the sustaining pedal has been the recording studio. As recording techniques have become more sensitive pianists have had to give more attention to the precise moment at which the pedal is depressed or raised:

In small rooms and on recordings, you can't use as much pedal as you can in Carnegie Hall.[64]

The greatest care is necessary when one is performing in an over-resonant hall. In a smallish room, less pedal is needed than in a large hall. Similarly with a 'full house', less minute attention is needed than in a hall which is sparsely filled. In broadcasting, pedalling must be somewhat restricted, as the microphone is particularly sensitive to the action of the pedals.[65]

Perhaps the greatest challenge of all in modern pedalling techniques lies in the new sounds and textures required by twentieth-century composers, most notably Debussy, Ravel and others in their 'school'. Early twentieth-century pedalling tutors devote considerable space to the problems of this style and later pedalling tutors usually contain a section or chapter on it. Debussy himself rarely marked the pedal – his markings can almost be counted on the fingers of both hands. Yet it is clear to anyone who is familiar with this style of piano music that the sustaining pedal must be used a great deal, and with enormous skill.

Despite all the attention given to the sustaining pedal in the twentieth century, it has seldom been notated with any precision in printed music. Plenty of suggestions have been made as to how this might be done[66] and some composers have gone to great lengths to ensure that their pedalling is as clear as possible (Ex. 67). This example, however, demonstrates at least one reason why more music does not contain detailed pedalling – it takes a lot of space and adds considerably to the cost of printing. Another reason, apparently given by Debussy, but echoed in a number of sources,[67] is the inability of any notation to meet the needs of every performing circumstance; pedalling changes according to the acoustics of a room, the presence of a microphone, etc.

Ex. 67 P. Grainger, 'Irish Tune from County Derry'

If it is possible to forgive composers and editors for omitting full pedalling in their scores, it is less easy to rationalise notation which is at best illogical and at worst misleading, in particular the use of rests in passages where the sustaining pedal remains depressed. This is not the preserve of just a few composers, or of one era. Composers as early as Beethoven and his contemporaries marked the use of the sustaining pedal at the same time as staccato dots and rests and composers and editors have been doing the same ever since. Is there in fact any difference between putting the sustaining pedal down and playing a note staccato and repeating the operation, only this time holding the note down with the finger as well? Many pianists would claim that there is, but the physical realities of the piano suggest otherwise. Once the hammer is travelling upwards towards the string under its own momentum the pianist no longer has any control over the sound until the dampers are brought into contact with the string. Whether the finger is removed quickly or slowly from the key makes no difference; unless, that is, there is a psychological difference between striking the key quickly, which might make a lighter, quieter sound, and holding the key down, which might produce a somewhat heavier hammer blow.

The use of the sustaining pedal has remained one of the most important aspects of piano performance; yet the issues surrounding it are as complex now as they have ever been, if not more so. This is true whether the performer plays on an early or modern instrument. Chopin's remark, that 'the correct employment of it remains a study of life'[68] is as true today as it was when it was first written.

9

Other pedals from c.1800

Soft pedals

A device for reducing the hammer blow from two strings to one is found at the very beginning of the piano's history on Cristofori's pianos. It is doubtful whether performers on these instruments thought of this device in the same way as later pianists, however: it was simply a remnant of harpsichord design akin to the mechanism which allowed a choice of one or two 8' registers. A similar mechanism has nevertheless persisted to the present day in the form of the una corda pedal.

Few hints as to the use of the una corda, or of any other type of soft pedal, stop or lever are to be found in eighteenth-century literature until the 1790s, and the evidence of the instruments themselves is somewhat ambivalent. On English grands, for example, the una corda was standard from Backers onwards (see Chapter 2). On 'Viennese' pianos, however, the situation was less clear. Walter included the moderator on his instruments; nevertheless when he introduced knee levers in place of hand stops, presumably for ease of use, the sustaining device benefited from the new system earlier than the moderator (see above, p. 18). Stein was more conservative, to begin with at least; there are no soft levers or stops on his earlier pianos (see above, p. 18). All this suggests that eighteenth-century pianists had only a limited need of any such device.

The three most important soft levers/pedals on grand pianos between c. 1790 and c.1830 were the lute, moderator and una corda. For the sake of clarity a brief description of each is given here.

Lute, moderator and una corda

The LUTE: (also know as 'harp' or 'buff') a strip of leather or some other material is pressed against the strings, inhibiting their vibration.

The MODERATOR: tongue-shaped pieces of leather or cloth are interposed between the hammers and strings, muffling the sound, but leaving the strings free to vibrate.

The UNA CORDA: the key action is shifted to the right and the hammers strike one or two strings only, the extent of the shift being regulated on some instruments (see above, p. 20).

This multiplication of soft pedals has given rise to some confusion over terminology. The term 'sourdine' was used in France for the lute ('Lautenzug' in Germany) whilst the moderator in Germany ('céleste' in France) was sometimes marked 'con sordino' or 'con sordini'.[1] In Germany the situation was further complicated by the presence of two moderators on some pianos. The degree of muting depended on the thickness of material interposed between the hammers and strings. The term 'pianissimo' could mean the more extreme form of moderator[2] (see on Schubert below), as could directions such as 'ppp sordino'. To complicate matters further, in the conventional notation associated with the 'Viennese' piano in the early nineteenth century 'con sordini' was the term for releasing the sustaining pedal, 'senza sordini' meaning 'raise dampers'. For the first few decades of the nineteenth century, 'sourdine' or 'sordino' ('sordini') might therefore refer to the lute, the moderator or the sustaining pedal, depending on geographical location and musical context. Later in the nineteenth century, and into the twentieth, yet another meaning emerged: 'sourdine' appears also to have been used sometimes to indicate the una corda after the other soft pedals had finally gone out of fashion (see below).

The use of each soft pedal varied from country to country. In France, Louis Adam devoted almost equal space to the lute and moderator in his discussion of the pedals common on grand pianos, but commented more briefly on the una corda (see the Appendix p. 172). In the musical examples that follow in his tutor only the moderator is used (usually in combination with the sustaining pedal). Most of these examples are in slow tempi, so that the absence of the lute is to be expected, since Adam has warned that it should only be used in fast passages. His avoidance of the una corda is more difficult to explain. Perhaps he disliked it because of the tuning problems it created when used in its extreme position where the hammer struck only one string with the same force normally used on all three. Or perhaps it was simply because the una corda was a relative newcomer amongst the pedals on French pianos, the lute, in particular, already having become established in the repertoire.

The use of the lute pedal in France

The lute pedal is specified in the two earliest works with printed pedalling – Steibelt's *6me Pot Pourri* and *Mélange* of 1793. In the first of these it is almost always combined with the sustaining pedal to characterise the recurring theme, which is played 'scherzando'. It is used alone only once, in a highly ornamented section which later appeared as an illustration in Milchmeyer's tutor.[3] In the *Mélange* it is used a little more extensively, but always in passage of fast notes and often with the sustaining pedal. The use of the lute pedal was not, however, restricted to trivial pieces in France at this time. Directions for the 'Sourdine' occur a number of times in Boieldieu's *Premier Concerto*, for example, again in passages of faster notes. It is also marked in a number of sonatas by composers such as Adam, H. Jadin, and Ladurner, all well-respected figures in Paris. This trend continued in the early years of the nineteenth century, in contrast to the absence of markings for the una corda in works by the same composers.

Dussek's reforming influence in Paris on his return there in 1807 has been discussed in Chapter 3. Whether this led to a change of attitude to the lute pedal is impossible to deduce. Chaulieu leads us to believe that Dussek's use of the pedals was restricted to just the sustaining pedal (see above p. 36), but he may have been over-stating the case since Dussek appears to indicate the lute in a set of variations on the 'March pour Tamerlane', where the directions 'sons Etouffés' and 'Sons liés' occur in the second variation. There is moreover clear evidence from Dussek's London years of his use of the una corda pedal (discussed below). Of the precise situation in Paris, however, we know very little. Evidently the lute remained popular in some quarters since piano makers continued to include it and some composers continued to specify it. But by c.1820 dissatisfaction with this rather unsubtle device was setting in:

As for the pedal which damps the vibrations by means of leather, it is not good in any case, since the fingers make the same effect without having the inconvenience of changing the tone-quality.[4]

Yet Erard patented a mechanism for it as late as 1827.[5] Soon after this, however, the device had sunk without trace, at least as far as the 'Paris' school was concerned:

The modern school has justly discarded the absurd taste which has uselessly complicated the system of *pedals*. They are now reduced to two.[6]

The use of the moderator and una corda by the Viennese school

Pianists of the Viennese school generally had a choice of two types of soft pedal – the moderator (sometimes with two thicknesses of material) and una corda. The una corda was a comparatively late addition to the Viennese piano. It did not occur at all in the eighteenth century and the impetus for its introduction probably came from imported English and French instruments, not least Haydn's Longman and Broderip piano, which he brought back from England in 1795, and the Erard pianos which both Haydn and Beethoven received as gifts in 1801 and 1803 respectively. A letter written by F. S. Silverstolpe states that the device was new on Walter's pianos in 1802:

The only commission of my Count that I have been able to execute is about the piano; but I flatter myself that I have done it well – I found one at the same instrument maker from whom I got the other one, that is, Walter. It is from the same wood and has the same outward look as the previous one but has great advantages as far as tone and strength are concerned. Usually each key has only two strings. But here there is a new and excellent invention: if one raises the left knee and activates a pedal, the key hits three strings all at once, by which one gets a forte that is superior to that of the earlier pianos, for now the tone (of the forte) is more like the piano tone and thus more natural. The invention was made long ago in England but was not imitated here till now . . .[7]

The details of this reference to the una corda are somewhat muddled; but it is clear that the author has this pedal in mind.

The moderator and una corda both found acceptance among Viennese pianists. Beethoven, in so many ways a member of the London school (in spirit at least), showed a characteristically early interest in the una corda in a letter of November 1802 to Nikolaus Zmeskall:

Reicha has been earnestly requested by the maker of his pianoforte to persuade me to let him make me one; and he is one of the more reliable ones, at whose firm I have already seen some good instruments – so you may give Walter to understand that, although I can have pianofortes for nothing from all the others, I will pay him 30 ducats, and on condition that the wood is mahogany. Furthermore, I insist that it shall have the *register (Zug) with one string* . . .[8]

Beethoven probably used the una corda in public as early as 1803; at least, that is what is implied by Czerny's account of Beethoven's performance of the slow movement from his Third Piano Concerto:

Beethoven . . . continued the pedal during the entire theme, which on the weak-sounding pianofortes of that day did very well, especially when the shifting (una-corda) pedal was also employed.[9]

The first markings for the una corda in Beethoven's music occur in the slow movement of the Fourth Piano Concerto, completed in 1806. He wrote at the beginning of the movement: 'throughout the entire *Andante* the pianist should apply the action-shifting (*una corda*) without interruption; otherwise the indication 'Ped.' refers to the usual (damper) pedal in accordance with present-day usage'.[10] Later in the movement the pianist is directed to release the una corda pedal gradually from 'una' through 'due e poi tre corde' and then to reverse the process within the space of six bars, the first of a number of similarly specific markings in Beethoven's later works. Some of the most detailed of these occur in the slow movement of the 'Hammerklavier' Sonata op. 106, which has about twenty markings for the una corda, including some which release the pedal progressively through the two-string stage. Sometimes the pedal is held down for lengthy stretches, for example at the beginning of the movement; on other occasions it is to be depressed for as little as one and a half bars. This implies that Beethoven was unconcerned about the inevitable change in tone-colour caused by this pedal, as well as its potential for putting the piano out of tune. Whether Beethoven was at all representative of early nineteenth-century pianists is uncertain; his hearing was beginning to deteriorate before he began to use the una corda to any extent, and he may therefore have been oblivious to some of the disadvantages recognised by other pianists (see below).

Beethoven's markings for the una corda pedal are much more numerous than most of his contemporaries' and he is most unusual in calling for the effect produced by progressively releasing the pedal from one to two, and then to three strings. The lack of directions for the moderator pedal in his music is particularly noteworthy, therefore suggesting that he did not like the device. It would be unwise to be too dogmatic, however, since the uneven spread of pedalling indications in Beethoven's later works suggests that he was far from consistent in marking their use.

Beethoven may have avoided the moderator in performance, but Schubert certainly did not. There are 'con sordino' or 'con sordini' markings in early and mature works by him. Many of these are in songs where they highlight a particular mood or effect, such as the direction at the beginning of 'Der Tod und das Mädchen' D531, a particularly sombre song, which reads 'Sempre con Pedale e Sordino'. Other markings occur in purely instrumental works. In the A minor Piano Sonata D748 there are several 'sordini' directions in the slow movement, usually of less than a bar's duration. All of them accompany a particular motif which is different in character from anything that surrounds it: the moderator simply serves to emphasise this character. In the Piano Sonata in D♭ major D567 there are two 'con sordini' markings, one each at the end of the exposition and development section of the first movement. There is less of a marked change in texture here than in the slow movement of the A minor sonata, but the moderator serves in this instance to emphasise two important structural moments. These and other similar markings in Schubert's music demonstrate a readiness to use the moderator pedal, but only in passages with a particular texture, with some structural significance or with some pictorial element. The inevitable change in timbre caused by this pedal does not lend itself to frequent, or incidental, use within a movement.

The direction 'durchaus mit dem Pianissimo' occurs at the beginning of the song 'Morgenlied' D685 in the autograph copy (but not in the first edition). It is the only such marking known to me in Schubert's music and may be an attempt on the composer's part to distinguish between the ordinary moderator pedal, normally marked 'sordini' or 'con sordini', and the additional, more extreme, form of the pedal found on some pianos. With this additional pedal a somewhat thicker piece of material was interposed between the hammers and the strings, making an even more muffled effect than usual. It was common enough on Viennese instruments and may have been the effect that Schubert had in mind. Some of the composer's other 'sordini' markings are accompanied by the direction 'ppp', however, so it remains far from certain that the 'Pianissimo' should be distinguished from the ordinary moderator. Schubert's direction for the una corda is 'mit Verschiebung', literally 'with shift' – an exact description of what happens when the pedal is depressed. As far as it is possible to tell from available sources, Schubert uses this direction only in music dated 1821 or later. Information concerning the instruments that he owned and played is sparse; but this may be an indication that he did not acquire an instrument with this pedal until relatively late in his career, despite the fact that Viennese pianos were equipped with them from the beginning of the century. Markings for the 'Verschiebung' occur in a number of places such as beginning of the Trio of the Piano Sonata in A minor D845 and in bar 51 of the second movement from the Piano Sonata in D major D850. It is also used in songs, such as 'Harfenspieler' I and III D478 and 480. Schubert's use of the una corda is analogous to his use of the moderator. It occurs at the beginning of sections, in passages where the texture is different, or for some illustrative reason. Nowhere does he indicate it in order to produce a gradual crescendo or diminuendo. In this respect his use of the device appears to differ significantly from Beethoven's in works published within very few years of each other. It is of course possible that Schubert marked this pedal only where he regarded it as absolutely essential, and that in his own performance he used it more freely in other places too; but there is a consistency in his moderator and una corda markings which suggests that he thought of both pedals as devices for changing the character of the piano's sound rather than assisting its dynamic capabilities.

The moderator remained in favour amongst pianists of the Viennese school rather longer than the lute pedal did in France. In the later 1830s, at the same time as Herz in Paris was dismissing all but the two pedals found on modern French grand pianos,[11] Czerny in Vienna was advocating a restricted use of the moderator:

This pedal is much seldomer used, even in Germany (where it is chiefly to be met with), than either of the two preceding kinds (the sustaining and una corda); and it is advantageously applicable only in a very soft *Tremando* on the lower octaves of the instrument, in conjunction with the Damper pedal, when it produces an imitation of distant thunder.[12]

A few years later, however, he had changed his mind. Commenting on Thalberg's op. 51, where the pedals are indicated, he remarks:

The words 'due pedali' signify that, besides the damper-pedal, we must here also employ that which moves the keyboard farther to the right, and by which the hammers are made to act upon one string. These are the only two pedals which are now found in good pianos, all others being acknowledged as unworthy of the true artist's notice.[13]

The una corda and the London school
In London there was no choice of soft pedals on grand pianos – the una corda was the only one – and there is ample evidence that it was used by the various

members of the London school. Some of this evidence is straightforward, such as the markings in the music itself, but other sources are more difficult to evaluate. Dussek presents us with perhaps the most intriguing problem of all. There are no 'una corda' markings anywhere in his piano music, but his *Instructions on the Art of Playing the Pianoforte or Harpsichord* (London and Edinburgh 1796) contains the following information:

MEZZO, to use the Pedal of the grand pianoforte, taking off only one string (p. 46)

A number of points are raised by this definition. How much of Dussek's music does it refer to: does it apply just to the music published in London following his arrival in that city from Paris in the 1780s? The una corda would have been known in France only from the imported grands and the absence of a similar definition in the French edition of the *Instructions*[14] suggests that the term 'Mezzo' could not have been understood there to mean una corda. Yet music by Dussek published in French editions contains as many instances of the term as English editions. This suggests that 'Mezzo' had more than one meaning in Dussek's mind; a suggestion which is reinforced by an examination of its use in Dussek's music. On page 8 of the first English edition of the Sonatas op. 14, for example, the sequence of directions 'f mezzo ppp' occurs within the space of three bars. The strong implication here is that 'Mezzo' is simply equivalent to 'mf' or 'mp'. Yet on the very same page, but in a different place, 'Mezzo' is used but is followed a few bars later by 'mf'. Should the performer assume that in this second case 'Mezzo' means 'una corda', but in the first case 'mf'? Alternatively, could it be that Dussek really meant the performer to depress the una corda pedal each time 'Mezzo' or its abbreviation occurs? If so, does 'Mezzo' mean 'two strings' and dynamics such as 'p' or 'pp' 'one string'? It is impossible to decide from an examination of the markings themselves.

The early nineteenth-century literature is scarcely more forthcoming. Chaulieu in his lengthy article on pedalling examined Dussek's technique of the sustaining pedal in detail, but referred to it as 'the only pedal that he chose to adopt'.[15] Such a dogmatic statement, that Dussek used *only* the sustaining pedal, cannot be accepted, however: he would hardly have recommended the use of the una corda in his tutor if this were the case. A clue to Dussek's style perhaps exists in the following comparison with Prince Louis Ferdinand, whose playing was apparently similar to Dussek's:

Dussek's playing is astonishingly accomplished, is sure, fiery, always effective – it is what is called now the grand style in order by this name to distinguish it from the *gallant*, elegant, delicate manner of playing (for example Himmel's). And such was the playing of Louis Ferdinand – only not so pure and clean as that of Dussek.[16]

Occasional indications for the una corda do exist in the works of Louis Ferdinand, which suggest that this teacher and companion of Dussek probably used it too.

The term 'Mezzo' was used by other members of the London school – Cramer for example, has 'mez', 'mezza voce', and 'mez:f' within a single publication – yet in none of the didactic material associated with the school (apart from Dussek's tutor) does a definition similar to Dussek's occur. One can only assume that other composers intended a dynamic (but not a pedal) effect by its use. This does not mean, however, that other members of the London school had no use for the una corda pedal. Whilst no mention of it is made in any music or didactic material by Clementi, it does occur in both sorts of literature by Cramer. His *Instructions for the Pianoforte* state that

the left hand pedal serves to move the keyboard from left to right, and takes off one or two strings from the hammers; it is chiefly used in Piano, Diminuendo, the Pianissimo passages. As the left hand pedal is only used in soft passages, it does not require any particular mark.[17]

Nevertheless, it is occasionally mentioned in his music. *A Grand March* (1799), for example, has at the beginning of its first movement, entitled 'Pastorelle', the direction:

NB. These marks ⊕ signify the right pedal must be used and these + where it is to be raised. The piano pedal must be kept down the chief part of this first movement and only raised when the ffor occurs.

The movement is two pages long and there are just five places where the direction 'ff' occurs, and then for chords of a single quaver's duration. The una corda should therefore be depressed for most of the movement. Similarly long stretches for which the pedal is held down feature in later works.

Cramer was clearly interested in the use of the una corda over a period of several years. What remains uncertain is whether he used it for passages of shorter duration, in brief diminuendos, for example. Did Cramer consider the resulting change of timbre an intrusion in these cases, or was he content to use the una corda as an additional dynamic effect over and above what could be accomplished with the fingers? The remarks in his *Instructions* do not specifically address all of these issues, but suggest that he may have used the una corda for shorter passages in some instances at least.

Another member of the London school, John Field, appears to have been very reserved in his use of the una corda. It seems not to have been his practice to mark it in his music and although comments on his technique are sparse, they tend to reinforce the view that he used it very little:

His use of the pedal was moderate. He never used the una-corda to play pp or diminuendo. The fingers did these.[18]

These remarks do not, however, rule out a use of the una corda in sections or passages where a change in timbre seems appropriate, such as some of the codas to his nocturnes.

Steibelt was not in London for long, but we have seen in earlier chapters how his arrival there coincided with the introduction of pedalling in printed editions. It comes as no surprise, therefore, to learn that his music contains a number of indications for the una corda, although his enthusiasm for it was qualified. Steibelt had made substantial use of the lute pedal in France, but when he arrived in England he encountered pianos with a different kind of soft pedal. This must have created a dilemma; should he replace the lute pedal markings of French editions with una corda directions when the same work was published in England? The editions themselves suggest that he was rather more circumspect. Imbault's edition of the second quintet from op. 28, for example, has the direction 'Servez vous de deux pédales ensemble celle qui leve les étouffoirs et l'autre qui fait la sourdine et vous aurez le son de la Harpe' (p. 26) ('Use both pedals together – that which raises the dampers and the other which makes the lute – and you will have the sound of the harp'). The parallel place in the English edition has only directions for the sustaining pedal.

There are some markings for the una corda in English editions of Steibelt's music. He referred to it simply as the 'soft pedal' and generally indicated it with the sign ⍓ . His use of it is not so extensive as his use of the lute, however – it is rarely used on more than a handful of occasions in any single work – but it is significant, and suggests that he was not unduly concerned about the change of timbre that it produced. In the Concerto op. 33 for example, it is used twice for just half a bar (Ex. 68), although it is more commonly indicated for three or more bars at a time in this and other works of the same period (Ex. 69).

The una corda is mentioned in some other piano tutors from early nine-teenth-century London, with degrees of enthusiasm ranging from toleration to disapproval:

One pedal is all that is necessary, namely, to raise the dampers while tuning.[19]

(Nicholson 1809)

This pedal being used only where the words Piano, Pianissimo, or their abbreviations piano, p. pp occur in a Musical Composition has not, and does not require any particular mark.[20]   (Jousse c. 1820)

The Pedal which moves the keys should never be used by a beginner.[21] (Crotch 1822)

If there are two pedals, this mark (Ped) means that on the right, the other being marked 'soft pedal' which is seldom used.[22]   (Burrowes 1834)

At least one author, Clarke, displayed remarkable ignorance in his comments:

The Pedal pressed by the left foot (on the Grand P. F.) is called the Piano, or Soft Pedal. It is generally signified by its name; and thus ⍓ when the foot is to be raised.[23]

(1830)

The sign which Clarke says indicates the release for the soft pedal is in fact the sign used by Steibelt to indicate where the pedal should be depressed.

Ex. 68 D. Steibelt, Concerto op. 33, first movement

⊕ denotes sustaining pedal

⟰ denotes una corda

✳ denotes pedal release

Ex. 69 D. Steibelt, Concerto op. 33, third movement

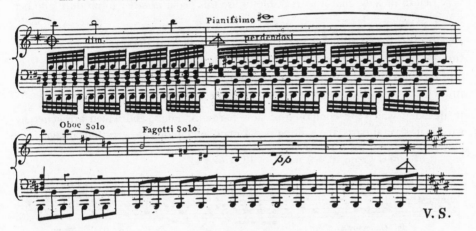

These tutors and the evidence associated with the major figures of the London school show how much opinions differed in London over the usefulness of the una corda. Some pianists can hardly have used it at all. Others reserved it for effects which required a particular timbre. A few, like Steibelt, saw it as a means of enhancing dynamic effects.

Subsequent developments in the use of the una corda

In 1896 Hipkins wrote:

Up to about 1830 there was a further shift permissible to one string only, the una corda of Beethoven; its employment was managed by a small hand-stop on one of the key blocks. In those days the hammers were small and of leather, and had much less blow, so that the wear was less than with the large felt hammers and powerful blow of the present day. The surface of the hammers now used would be much cut up by the practice of a double shift for ordinary service.[24]

Hipkins's estimated date for the disappearance of the true una corda is slightly early – it lived on well into the 1830s[25] – but his account of the reasons for its demise is a reminder that the nature of the instrument itself was changing rapidly during the first decades of the century. The change of hammer covering from leather to felt, and the increasing size of the hammer head itself, posed problems for the use of the una corda, which a number of writers articulated:

There is little to say on the subject of the pedal which moves the keyboard, except that it is wise never to play loudly when it is used, as one runs the risk of putting the piano out of tune.[26]   (Zimmerman 1840)

In rapid passages, however, this pedal ought not to be used, as it is deficient in the requisite energy.[27]   (Fétis and Moscheles 1837)

In making use of this pedal we must take care not to play too hard, as the single strings are easily put out of tune or even broken . . . it is only in a few passages, very rich in melody, that it is desirable to use this pedal in order to produce another species of tone.[28]   (Czerny 1838–9)

Because of these problems very few pianists followed Beethoven's example in the use of the progressive una-due-tre corde effect. Czerny includes the effect among the musical examples accompanying his comments on the use of the una corda (Ex. 70), but even he expressed some caution:

In melodies which are composed of slow harmonic notes, and which are generally written in several parts, the shifting pedal may be employed to great advantage.

Ex. 70 C. Czerny op. 500, trans., vol. III, p. 64

. . . This pedal must however be but sparingly employed, and the player must not think that every Piano passage is to be produced by means of this pedal.

    The most beautiful and honourable kind of piano will always be that, which is produced by the fingers alone, and by a light and delicate touch.[29]

Nevertheless the use of the una corda continued to be recommended, albeit with reservations. Even the conservative Hummel allowed it in places:

Though a truly great artist has no occasion for pedals to work upon his audience by expression and power, yet the use of the damper pedal, combined occasionally with the piano pedal (as it is termed), has an agreeable effect in many passages.[30]

He was by no means alone in recommending the use of the una corda with the sustaining pedal. Herz, for example, commented:

The una corda or soft pedal is rarely employed alone; but, united with the loud pedal, it produces very beautiful effects.[31]

In general, however, pianists of the post-Beethoven and London school era regarded the una corda pedal with some suspicion. Only one tutor speaks wholeheartedly in favour of it: the *Méthode* of Friedrich Kalkbrenner, a pupil of Louis Adam who spent most of his performing life in Paris:

[The una corda] produces a marvellous effect in all diminuendo passages, and may be used when a composer has marked a diminuendo, morendo, or piannissimo.[32]

A large number of markings for the una corda are found in Kalkbrenner's music – far more than in that by any of his better-known contemporaries. They reveal an idiosyncratic technique whereby the ends of sections or movements are often accompanied by the use of the una corda (Ex 71).

Ex. 71 F. Kalkbrenner, 24 Preludes op. 88 no. 12

With Kalkbrenner's technique we see the beginnings of a 'Parisian' style of una corda pedalling that was to prove unacceptable to some. This style was caricatured by Wieck some years later in a chapter which follows immediately on his denunciation of Parisian excesses in the use of the sustaining pedal (see p. 106 above):

Chapter VI

The Soft-Pedal Sentiment

You exclaim: 'What is that? – a sentiment for the soft pedal! a sentiment of any kind in our times! most of all, a musical sentiment! I have not heard of such a thing in the concert-room for a long time!

When the foot-piece to the left on the piano is pressed down, the key-board is thereby moved to the right, so that, in playing, the hammers strike only two of the three strings, in some pianos only one. In that way the tone is made weaker, thinner, but more singing and more tender. What follows from this? Many performers, seized with a piano madness, play a bravoura piece, excite themselves fearfully, clatter up and down through seven octaves of runs, with the pedal constantly raised, – bang away, put the best piano out of tune in the first twenty bars, – snap the strings, knock the hammers off their bearings, perspire, strike the hair out of their eyes, ogle the audience, and make love to themselves. Suddenly they are seized with a sentiment! They come to a *piano* or *pianissimo*, and, no longer content with one pedal, they take the soft pedal while the loud is still resounding. Oh what languishing! what tenderness of feeling! what a soft-pedal sentiment! The ladies fall into tears, enraptured by the pale long-haired artist.

I describe here the period of piano mania, which has just passed its crisis; a period which it is necessary to have lived through, in order to believe in the possibility of such follies.[33]

Wieck, writing in 1853, perhaps makes a thinly veiled reference to Liszt ('the pale, long-haired artist'), but his comments apply more generally to the style of piano playing associated with Paris in the 1830s and 1840s. Clearly this school of playing represented one extreme. Wieck, on the other hand, represented the opposite extreme. Even pianists whom he considered to be 'rational players' went too far in their use of the una corda, in his opinion:

Even they use the soft pedal too much and too often and at unsuitable places; for instance, in the midst of a piece, without the preparatory pause; in melodies which require to be lightly executed; or in rapid passages which are to be played piano. This is especially to be noticed with players who are obliged to use instruments of a powerful tone and stiff, heavy action, on which it is difficult to insure a delicate shading in *piano* and *forte*.[34]

'The preparatory pause' referred to here is explained a little further on by Wieck:

The soft pedal may be used in an echo; but should be preceded by a slight pause, and then should be employed throughout the period, because the ear must accustom itself gradually to this tender, maidenly, sentimental tone. There must then again be a slight pause before the transition to the more masculine tone, with the three strings.[35]

This advice excludes the use of the una corda for simple dynamic effects such as those advocated by Kalkbrenner, and reserves it for discrete sections in which a new tone quality is required, a situation which must have limited the una corda's use very severely. At least one other contemporary of Wieck's held similar views, but expressed them much more succinctly: in 1844 Joseph Wade wrote (ironically in a volume dedicated to Franz Liszt) 'The sudden use of this pedal should be avoided.'[36]

By the middle of the nineteenth century attitudes towards the una corda were similar to, though not identical with, those towards the sustaining pedal. The 'progressive' pianists were associated with Paris and the 'conservatives' with elements of the German tradition, while most other pianists no doubt occupied the middle ground. But as with the sustaining pedal, there were substantial differences even among the chief representatives of the Paris school during the second quarter of the nineteenth century.

Thalberg

Thalberg's use of the una corda can be judged by the relatively extensive markings of it in his scores. Typically, there are one or two indications in each piece, presumably in places where the una corda was essential in all circumstances for the effect, but the true extent of its use can be seen in the transcriptions in his tutor, *L'Art du chant*, from which Example 72 is taken. Here we have evidence of a technique which is apparently unconcerned with the change of timbre resulting from the use of the una corda, and in which the pedal is depressed for as little as two beats at a time: in this case to shade the end of a phrase in a manner highly reminiscent of Kalkbrenner. These markings accord with Marmontel's description of Thalberg's playing, in which he says that 'Thalberg constantly used the soft and loud pedals in an alternating and simultaneous manner.'[37] Marmontel was a discriminating critic who said of another pianist, Gottschalk, that 'he used the una corda pedal perhaps too often;'[38] but he evidently saw nothing wrong with Thalberg's pedalling. Indeed, far from detracting from the expressiveness of his performance of slower pieces, the una corda seems only to have heightened the effect, and according to at least one other author: 'Thalberg's soft playing was exquisitely tender and touching.'[39]

Thalberg's markings for the una corda have given rise to some confusion over terminology. He frequently used the term 'con sordini' or 'con sordino', which some have taken to mean the moderator:

The use of the pianissimo mute [moderator] was indicated by the Italian word 'Sordino'. Mr Franklin Taylor has pointed out to the writer the use of this term in the sense of a mute as late as Thalberg's op. 41.[40]

Rosamund Harding took up a similar, though not identical, interpretation of the marking, citing Thalberg's op. 42 as an example.[41] Thalberg's op. 41 and 42 were published in 1841 or 1842; but if the markings in them refer to the lute, as Harding suggests, or the moderator, as Hipkins supposed, they represent an extremely late use of those pedals in view of contemporary comments in tutors already referred to (see p. 136 above). A pianist in the early 1840s could have played a fifteen-year-old piano with both lute and moderator; but a performer of Thalberg's stature would surely have performed on the most

Ex. 72 S. Thalberg, *L'Art du chant*, piano transcription no. 4

up-to-date instruments with just two pedals. If this was the case, his 'con sordini' markings on opp. 41 and 42 cannot have been for the lute or moderator. Furthermore, these two works were not in fact the last in which these markings occurred. 'Con sordino' indications can be found as late as op. 77 (c. 1862), by which time it is inconceivable that a pianist of Thalberg's stature would be using the lute or moderator. This work is particularly interesting because it is the only example of which I am aware which has both 'con sordino' and 'una corda' markings. In one place they occur within two bars of each other (Ex. 73). This is admittedly unusual, and demonstrates a somewhat casual approach to the notation; but it could hardly be taken to mean the use of the lute or moderator for two bars, followed immediately by a change of timbre for the una corda, especially as the passage is repeated a few bars later with the una corda depressed throughout.

Ex. 73 S. Thalberg, *Grande Fantaisie de Concert* op. 77, p. 4

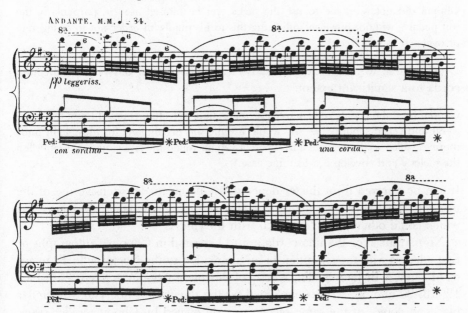

Thalberg was not the only composer to indicate the una corda with 'con sordino' or 'con sordini' markings. Several French composers adopted the same, or similar, terminology. Alkan, for example, uses 'Sordamente' or simply 'Sourd' in some places, although the una corda is mostly used with the sustaining pedal in his works, in which case the direction 'due pedale' is used. Ravel also uses the term, in *Gaspard de la nuit* for example, which includes the direction 'Sourdine durant toute la piece' at the beginning of 'Le Gibet'. Similar markings can be found in works by other composers, and the term occasionally appears in literature throughout the twentieth century:

sordine, E., Sordino . . . con s. In piano-playing 'use the soft pedal'.[42]

second (left, 'sordinen'-) pedal (which can also be indicated by 'una corda').[43]

UNA CORDA. . . . term used on the piano to indicate the use of the left pedal, called 'sourdine' pedal, or soft pedal.[44]

Chopin

Thalberg's use of the una corda pedal may have been acceptable to most who heard him, but to at least one of his professional colleagues, Chopin, it was not refined enough; 'he produces *piano* with the pedal instead of with the hand'.[45] This offers a clue as to Chopin's own technique of the una corda, which was evidently very refined. His advice to pupils was 'learn to make a *diminuendo* without the help of the [una corda] pedal; you can add it later'.[46] Another account (also quoted on p. 127 above) emphasises just how cautious he was over its use:

Chopin did not want me to use the pedal, yet he himself used it, particularly the soft pedal – without however indicating this to his pupils, in order not to exaggerate or overstep its resources.[47]

Despite these words of caution, it is clear that Chopin did rely on the una corda to a significant extent:

Chopin used the pedals with marvellous discretion. He often coupled them to obtain a soft and veiled sonority . . . he would use the soft pedal alone for those light murmurings which seem to create a transparent vapour round the arabesques that embellish the melody and envelop it a like fine case.[48]

It can be inferred from this evidence that Chopin made extensive use of the una corda, but never as a matter of course or simply to obtain a dynamic effect which could otherwise be achieved with the fingers.

No markings for the una corda are to be found in Chopin's autographs or first editions with the exception of an annotation to the Nocturne in F♯ major op. 15 no. 2. In Jane Stirling's copy of this piece Chopin marked '2' in bars 12, 18, 20 and 58. This is explained by the direction 'i due Ped.' in similar places in copies of the same piece formerly owned by Chopin's older sister, although the directions are not in Chopin's hand.[49] These markings are sufficient to show that Chopin had few reservations about introducing the una corda into the middle of a phrase, and that he used it for brief passages of a few beats on occasion.

Liszt and his German and Austrian contemporaries

Liszt's use of the una corda is impossible to describe in detail; there is simply not enough evidence. Friedrich Wieck's comments (see p. 146 above) suggest that Liszt made extensive use of it and there are at least some markings for it in his music, especially in the later works. They are almost invariably of several bars' duration, and presumably therefore indicate those places where Liszt wanted a particular effect, rather than every occurrence in his own performances. A good example is his B minor Sonata. The direction 'una corda' occurs in bar 329, followed a few bars later by 'sempre una corda'; but these are the only markings for either pedal in the work; they suggest that

Liszt wanted a particular effect in this instance, without precluding the possibility of the una corda's use elsewhere in the piece.

If Thalberg, Chopin and Liszt made extensive use of the una corda, just as they had introduced bold effects with the sustaining pedal, it is equally likely that many of their German and Austrian contemporaries were much more restrained. Friedrich Wieck certainly was, but what about the younger members of his school? Markings for the una corda occasionally occur in Robert Schumann's works, in most cases for passages of several bars' duration. But if his playing resembled his wife's to any degree, we can be fairly certain that he used the una corda extremely selectively, since Clara Schumann was almost as outspoken on the subject as her father. Rubinstein in particular caused her to write in strong terms. On one occasion he was described as having 'no sentiment but that of the soft pedal'.[50]

Another time, she wrote:

Rubinstein gave a concert that night and I went to it; but I was furious, for he no longer plays, either there is a perfectly wild noise or else a whispering with the soft pedal down – and a would-be cultured audience puts up with a performance like this.[51]

Mendelssohn, another member of the Schumann circle, included some markings in his music. Ten per cent or so of his scores contain indications for the una corda, although most of these works have only one or two. It is impossible to tell from these markings alone whether Mendelssohn followed Wieck in allowing the una corda only for whole passages which required a distinct timbre, or during phrases for a beat or two, as appears to have been the case with Thalberg, Chopin and probably Liszt.

The una corda and moderator in pedalling tutors

The una corda receives scant treatment in the pedalling tutors of the late nineteenth and twentieth centuries. Schmitt, the first author to write comprehensively on the sustaining pedal, devoted no more than half a page to the una corda in his book. This is mostly description of the mechanism rather than advice on its use. Indeed, his description of the una corda suggests that he had very little experience of it, a remarkable fact for one who had apparently investigated the technique of the sustaining pedal so minutely:

In grand pianos its effect is to cause a slight movement of the keyboard to the right, in consequence of which the hammer strikes one string, or sometimes two, instead of three . . .[52]

There can surely have been very few grand pianos less than thirty years old at the time Schmitt was writing whose una corda pedals caused the hammers to strike just one string. The vast majority would have had the 'due corde' pedals, similar to those on modern grands, a fact of which Schmitt seems curiously unaware. Schmitt's advice on the use of the una corda is limited to two practical observations: if used 'too frequently the effect is cloying', and 'care must be taken not to play forte, since the single string cannot bear as strong a blow as the three.[53]

Rather surprisingly, Schmitt devotes more space to the moderator than he does to the una corda. It seems that Bösendorfer's had recently revived this pedal on grand pianos and that it had been 'repeatedly used in concerts with such success that no uninitiated hearer suspected the employment of any especial contrivance'. Its use in the concert hall is not discussed by other writers so its revival in performance can only have been short-lived, but as a 'practice pedal', for 'all monotonous but necessary exercises'[54] the moderator is mentioned in a number of later sources.

After Schmitt the una corda received slightly better treatment in other pedalling tutors. Some of them describe its action in detail, explaining how its effect is achieved as much by bringing a softer, less worn, part of the hammer covering into contact with the string, as by reducing the number of strings struck by the hammer. Most of them concentrate on the different timbre produced by the una corda rather than the question of volume. Bowen discusses these elements at length and sums up the advice found in most twentieth-century tutors which deal with the subject.

The portions of the hammer facings which have not been used so much (between the grooves and at the sides) remain in a softer and more 'cushiony' condition, and as it is arranged that upon depressing the pedal the hammers strike the strings on this comparatively unused surface, we get the effect and colour we should get from soft hammers, and a more velvety tone is the result.

It is this, emphatically, that makes the U.C. attachment so valuable, and not merely the fact that the volume of tone is reduced.

If we treat the keys correctly we can produce a perfect pianissimo on three strings, so that actually we should regard our soft pedal as a splendid means of changing the colour of our tone, and use it artistically for that purpose − not casually for the mere sake of playing softly. It is this misconception of its value that leads to the thoughtless abuse so often indulged in where perhaps at every sight of 'piano' or 'diminuendo' the left foot is plunged down, regardless of the sudden change of tone quality, which makes the effect very patchy. Yes, indeed, the soft pedal should be regarded as a mute, and discerning care taken to put it on − or off − at a suitable moment in the phrasing, and not in the middle of a phrase or passage.[55]

Similar remarks are made by others with varying degrees of scepticism and reservation which suggest that modern pianists are far from convinced about the merits of the una corda pedal.

The sostenuto pedal

By the time a viable mechanism for a selective tone-sustaining device had been developed (see Chapter 2, p. 23) pianists had developed a highly sophisticated technique of the conventional sustaining pedal which already enabled them, for example, to sustain a bass note while at the same time damping out unwanted notes in higher registers by means of half-pedalling. It is no wonder, therefore, that instructions in pedalling tutors for the use of the sostenuto pedal are usually relegated to the final pages of a volume, mostly as an after-thought. It barely receives any mention at all in Schmitt's tutor. He describes its introduction on pianos by Steinway of New York and Ehrbar of Vienna and adds:

It was designed to give an explicit and detailed account of these various devices for the prolongation of especial tones, but space failing, they can only receive mention in this connection. Should it be desired, a more thorough review of them will be published at some future time.[56]

No such review appeared, but at about the same time as Schmitt was writing his tutor, Liszt encountered Steinway's sostenuto pedal on a piano sent to him by the firm. He wrote thanking Steinway's for the gift and expressed interest in the sostenuto pedal, even including two examples to demonstrate how it might be used in his own music.[57] This suggests that Liszt might have used the pedal with some enthusiasm, had it been available in his younger days; but it arrived far too late in his career to have any significant impact.

Other pianists and teachers at the end of the nineteenth century appear to have been slow to adopt the sostenuto pedal, as far as it is possible to tell. Schmitt's brief reference to it might have inspired later writers to take it up, and to offer suggestions for its use; but it receives no mention at all in the major European pedalling treatises of that era, by Köhler, Lavignac and Rubinstein. The scepticism with which the device was viewed has already been described in Chapter 2. The prevailing attitude was summed up by Hipkins:

It has again been brought forward by Steinway and others, and its value much insisted upon. We cannot however believe that it will be of use in a concert room.[58]

It comes as no surprise to learn, therefore, that the first detailed exposition of the sostenuto pedal is found in an American source, the Pedal Method by Albert Venino (New York 1893):

A few words in reference to the sustaining [sostenuto] pedal, which is destined to become of great value to the pianist, will not be amiss. It is found between the damper and soft pedal, and will sustain a note or chord, but will not sustain runs of any kind. The third or sustaining pedal, (unlike its many short-lived predecessors), has come to stay; although it has not received universal recognition yet, because but few piano manufacturers have applied it to their instruments. In the concert room it has scarcely been used at all, perhaps because pianists have not fully realised its importance. While it is true that there are comparatively few instances where it can be applied in our past and present piano music, there is no doubt that its importance will influence future composers.

ITS USE

81 This pedal is applied when it is desirable to sustain a single tone or chord exclusively, and must be pressed down *after* the key (keys) has been struck, but before it has been released. It is only affected by the soft and damper pedals when they have preceded it. In the few examples given here the pupil will perceive the advantage gained by using the sustaining pedal. The tone sustained by the third pedal enables the performer to change the damper pedal as often as necessary, or dispense with it altogether, without affecting the sustained tone . . . [there then follow four written examples of cases where the sustaining pedal's use is beneficial in the existing repertoire.]

85 Bach's A minor organ prelude, transcribed for the piano by Liszt, is a most interesting example for the 'sustaining pedal'. The A in the bass needs to be sustained for more than a page, but in what way? The damper pedal can under no circumstances be used. The sustaining pedal, if used immediately after striking the A, will also catch the C above it and sustain that also. To make a slight pause in the upper voices and strike the 'A' alone would probably answer; but, at the same time, cause a break in the upper voices, which would hardly justify the means employed. The only proper manner is silently to press down the A before beginning the prelude and hold it with the sustaining pedal. Do not raise the foot until the Organ-point A has ended. In this manner, the desired effect will be obtained. (pp. 45–7)

Venino in this passage concentrates on the use of the sostenuto in a work not originally intended for the piano (as had Liszt in one of the examples he sent to Steinway). But elsewhere he discusses its use in original piano works, showing how this pedal was at last beginning to find its way into the performance of the standard repertoire – a trend culminating in Banowetz's extensive chapter on the subject.[59]

There are few markings for the sostenuto pedal in printed music, most of them by American composers such as Barber, Carter, Copland, Harris and Sessions. In general, however, the sostenuto has been avoided by European pianists and composers.

'Toy pedals'

One of the fascinations of the recent revival of interest in early pianos has been the array of pedals on some of the more lavish early nineteenth-century models. But how much notice should the modern pianist take of these devices in the performance of mainstream repertoire? The answer is simple – not very much. First of all, 'bassoon' and 'Turkish music' pedals were not available throughout Europe (see Chapter 2) – barely at all in Britain. Secondly, the more extreme effects (drums, cymbals, triangle) were only included on a few extravagant instruments. The pianos owned or played by the more influential pianists and composers did not include them. Thirdly, markings for them do not occur in works by 'better' composers – apart from the occasional indiscretion such as Hummel's marking for the bassoon pedal.[60] Finally, the serious, 'professional' tutors are outspoken in their condemnation of them. Fétis, looking back over the early history of the piano, noted that:

Several other essays were made to improve the construction of square pianos; and under the impossibility of attaining it, recourse was had to an augmentation of the number of pedals, the object of which was to modify the quality of sounds. But these factitious means of producing effect were held but in little account by distinguished artists and true amateurs.[61]

Hummel (despite his bassoon pedal markings) wrote:

All other pedals [in addition to the 'damper' and 'piano' pedals] are useless, and of no value to the performer or to the instrument.[62]

Czerny began his discussion of the pedals by commenting 'Among the several kinds that have at different times been introduced, the three following are necessary to the player'. This is followed by a discussion of the sustaining, moderator and una corda pedals. He concluded by adding:

All other pedals, as the Fagotto and Harp pedals, or the Drum and Bells, or Triangle, &c. are childish toys of which a solid player will disdain to avail himself.[63]

The modern performer might perhaps contemplate using one of these pedals in a work of a less serious nature, but it would be altogether inappropriate, for example, to use them in a sonata or concerto. These devices may be of historical interest, but they are not of enormous practical value. Schmitt summed it up well:

Besides the damper pedal,the old pianos frequently possessed others; e g, one which imitated the bassoon; another, the great drum – which was effected by a blow on the sounding board; a bell pedal; one to imitate cymbals and other such infantile contrivances, now happily obsolete.[64]

Chapters on pedalling from piano tutors

J. P. Milchmeyer, *Die wahre Art das Pianoforte zu spielen* (Dresden 1797)

Chapter 5 (pp. 57 – 66)
Understanding the piano and its mutation(s)*

In large towns, there are always many craftsmen who make pianos and you have a choice. Nevertheless, I now advise every amateur who wishes to purchase a piano that he shouldn't balk at the thought of paying 20 – 30 thaler. A good instrument is like a fine painting, and likewise is worth two or three times as much after the death of the master. If you are able to choose between various types of instruments, I would recommend that greater preference be given to the small, square piano. The grand piano takes up more space, is more expensive to take around on journeys, and has fewer mutations than the square, even though these mutations produce so many effects and gain ever-increasing approval. In the case of grand pianos, I have also found that the two highest octaves seldom have a proportionately beautiful, resonant and incisive tone; the bass notes are more often than not extraordinarily strong and the upper notes thin, so that an instrument of this kind resembles a gentleman in a poor suit accompanied by a magnificently clothed servant, or a large man, seven feet tall, whose voice resembles that of a child. If the tone and mutations of grand pianos were correspondingly more beautiful than those of the square, I would be the first to recommend them, but as yet I have very seldom found this to be the case, and I therefore find myself having to return to the little square, and when investigating its excellence, pointing out features that we have just observed.

First of all, when examining a piano, the player must listen very attentively [to establish] whether the notes are clear and the resonance is of long duration when he plays and sustains a chord in the uppermost register, for in this way, an assessment can be made of the quality of the soundboard; then, whether these notes resemble a beautiful female voice, graduating just a little into the tone of a clarinet. After this, you [should] play the notes slowly one after the other from the top to the bottom and note carefully whether they vary at all

* (Translator's footnote) The terms used by Milchmeyer for tone-modifying devices and their effects do not always have English equivalents. In this translation 'Veränderungen' is translated as 'mutations', 'Zug' as 'register', leaving 'pedal' only for those places where Milchmeyer specifically mentions it.

in quality; whether, for example, some sound too harsh, some too velvety, and others too dull. Throughout, all the notes must be of one and the same quality, and when played separately one after the other from top to bottom, each note must be almost imperceptibly, I might say, just a shade, quieter than the one immediately above; thereby the notes of the treble clef, which nearly always have the melodic line, are heard in their full splendour. You must not imitate the practice of those who, when trying out an instrument, play chords merely to discover whether it has a good bass. Strong notes are only useful when accompanying an orchestra in a concert hall or opera house. Also in earlier styles of music they were necessary; but in modern music, a strong bass is less essential than a clear, abundantly sonorous and resonant treble, so that the many beautiful passages with which composers of the past twenty years have enriched our [music], can be played with taste and perfection. When all the notes are played *pianissimo* with and without the dampers, the hammers must never falter, and none of the notes, when played with the same pressure, should sound weaker or stronger than the others. In the case of the *fortissimo*, the hammers must not rebound and produce a disagreeable, metallic noise. Furthermore, it goes without saying that even in the pianissimo, a certain amount of weight or percussive action from the fingers, an absolute prerequisite of piano playing, must be applied; and also that, on the contrary, no excessive force should be used in the *fortissimo*. When you have completed this test, you very quickly repeat [the notes] several times to see whether the hammers falter. Also after that, you note whether the action of the keys is too heavy or whether they fall too deeply since both [weaknesses] are a hindrance to fast playing. Then you examine the keys themselves. The black keys must be neither too wide nor too short, because if they are too wide, people with particularly large fingers would not be able to play between them, which is so necessary in modern music; if they are too short, the player with a rather large hand has constantly to bend his fingers too much, and is thereby hindered in his performance, or is endlessly knocking against the board at the back of the keys with his fingers and nails. With regard to the white or lower keys, it should be observed that they are not too short, and that their edges have not been cut too sharply. In the first case, the hand easily slips off while playing; in the second, the player runs the danger of injuring his fingers when playing quickly. You now turn to the dampers and check whether they damp all the notes effectively, especially those of the lowest bass register, and whether some perhaps do not just touch a third string, which is harmful to the tone of the other note. In the case of every single damper, you should also note carefully whether the sound ends abruptly without leaving an unpleasant vibration or hiss, and whether some dampers perhaps remain slightly in contact [with the strings] when they are raised by the pedal. With regard to the harp or leather register, which acts upon the strings from below, I must recommend you to ascertain whether it lies evenly from top to bottom, and operates in such a way that the upper strings are not damped too much or the lower ones too little. Also, with this register, the balance of the upper and lower notes must remain [unaffected], and the treble notes even here must retain their brilliance. In the case of the mutation that causes each hammer to strike one string only, you should notice especially whether the notes remain in tune, for I have often observed that some notes sound out of tune and therefore render this mutation useless. As regards the lid [of the instrument], it should not move in an irregular or jerky manner but quite smoothly, and there should be no noise when it closes. Of the four pedals, two should always be installed in such a way that they can be put down with one foot; thus all four can be operated by the two feet. All the pedals should be arranged in one [straight] line, and none of them should go down further or with greater difficulty than the others. Furthermore they should operate very smoothly and produce no squeaking or creaking noises. Above all, you should examine the soundboard minutely, [and note] whether it is durably made without cracks and flaws, and whether the bridge is perfectly glued. Regarding the tuning pins, you must notice whether they tend to slope towards the keyboard and whether the holes have been more deeply bored than is necessary; for if the pins project through the wood, the instrument cannot remain in tune for a single instant; then you must also notice whether the strength of the tuning pins is commensurate with that of the strings: whether, for example, the pins of the bass notes are too weak, for this too would interfere with the steadiness of the tuning; and whether there are any round or twisted pins, because these can no longer be turned, making it impossible to tune them. Rusty strings likewise cannot be tolerated on the instrument. They always sound out of tune and are constantly liable to snap. I would therefore advise every owner of a good instrument to allow others to touch the strings as little as does he himself, since the least moisture causes them to rust, to go out of tune and then to break. Furthermore, nothing at all should lie or be placed on the instrument; generally speaking, a good instrument is as valuable and needs to be cared for as much as your eyes, and for that reason, it must not be touched by any clumsy players.

The old custom of placing a drawer beneath the instrument in which to store music is quite objectionable, for anyone can easily understand that the constant pulling out and pushing in of the drawer must disturb the instrument and put it out of tune. When you buy a new instrument, do ask its maker at the time to write down the actual gauge of each string alongside the tuning pin and to give you the name of the maker from whom he acquired them, for the good tone of an instrument depends entirely on a genuine and exactly matching set of strings. Even the base of the piano needs to be inspected, for if it is too thin, the instrument will warp in time and assume a concave shape. If a square piano measures up to these criteria, then it is worth buying; and to keep a good instrument properly maintained, a player who practises a great deal should have the hammers re-glued every three years preferably by the maker of the instrument himself, or at least by another skilful instrument maker; he should also have the springs of the dampers checked to see whether any of them have become a little brittle or are completely broken.

If you live in a region or town where only grand pianos are made, then you must clearly make do with one of those and, before buying it, subject it to the same inspection that I have recommended for square pianos. Anyone who is too poor to buy a piano must content himself with a clavichord, for, next to the piano, this is the [keyboard] instrument most susceptible to musical expression. The harpsichord is the only one that I cannot in any way recommend. The rules that I have expounded in the preceding few chapters are equally applicable to the clavichord.

As far as the mutations are concerned, we cannot praise instrument makers sufficiently for their unstinting efforts in recent years to introduce a large number of different mutations into the instrument. But they have seldom been used sufficiently by players and thus resemble a fine collection of books that no one ever reads. Composers and teachers ignored them, and regarded them as unnecessary, until finally the great talent of Steibelt, a Berliner by birth but now residing in London, developed all these mutations carefully, demonstrated the effect of each one and defined its function. In the following analyses and description of the piano's mutations, I will therefore take my examples from passages and melodies written by this composer. All the music of this great composer, his sonatas as well as his pot-pourris, is perfectly suited to the piano. But certainly, with regard to expression and necessary knowledge of the instrument, it requires the greatest perfection in performance and is like a fine tragedy that must be well performed if it is to achieve its fullest effect. In a word, the music of this great composer, who is a real credit to his home town of Berlin, requires the most perfect performance on the very best instrument.

I come now to the mutations themselves and begin with the harp or leather register. This consists of a piece of thick, soft leather which is applied to the strings and thereby inhibits them, so that when they are struck, they do not vibrate quite as much, thus giving the instrument a muffled tone. In slow pieces which require a soft, sustained and resonant tone, this stop cannot be used; all the better, however, is it suited to pieces of a cheerful or playful character, to many a pastoral song, and to siciliano-like compositions. Mordents and short trills have a delightful effect with this stop; also, certain solo passages in the bass sound excellent with it. The first example below shows the use of the leather stop with the piano lid closed, the other with the lid down. All pedal effects that are marked with a cross may also be achieved on a grand piano [Exx. 74, 75].

Ex. 74

Ex. 75

There is much to say concerning the dampers; they can create either the most beautiful effect or the most abominable, depending on whether they are used with taste or bad judgement. In the latter case, all the notes sound together and produce such a horrible cacophony that you want to cover your ears. I will therefore provide several examples to illustrate the use of this mutation.

Firstly, you can imitate little bells with it when the right hand plays detached notes, *mezzo forte* in a fairly high register, while the left provides an accompaniment in the middle of the keyboard, *legato* and *pianissimo*.

Ex. 76

If, in a slow movement, the right hand plays the accompaniment *pianissimo* and *legato*, and a melody is given out, *mezzo forte*, in the bass and the whole passage is performed without the dampers and with the lid closed, you can very effectively represent a duet for two men accompanied by an instrument. Whenever the right hand plays alone, the lid can be opened and closed to increase and reduce the volume of sound.

Ex. 77

To imitate a duet sung by male and female voices accompanied by a violin, the hammers which play the violin accompaniment of the right hand must only vibrate [lightly] against the strings. If these same notes occur very quickly one after another, the keys, after they have been put down for the first time in the usual manner, must subsequently be raised only half as high. In slow pieces, this method of pedalling has a very fine effect. Moreover, the right hand must nearly always play *pianissimo* and the left hand in the bass, *mezzo forte*. If the latter is passed over the right to imitate the female voice, it plays *forte* with the lid raised.

Ex. 78

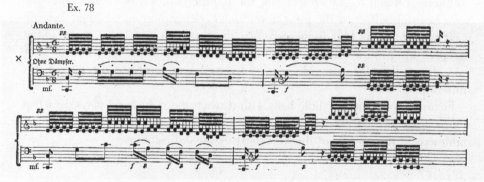

When the right hand plays *mezzo forte* without the dampers and with the lid closed, a long held note can be effectively sustained by rapid repetition [of a note] or by allowing the hammer to vibrate against the string, thus imitating a female voice; here, however, the left hand must play the bass *mezzo forte* and the accompaniment *pianissimo*. With this mutation, because of the cacophony that results from the combined resonance of the notes, you have to damp the last note of the chord and begin the first notes of the following chords without the dampers.

Ex. 79

To produce a great *crescendo*, representing the rising sun, clouds dispersing or the like, you should begin *pianissimo* without the dampers and with the lid closed. As the *fortissimo* is reached, you raise the lid little by little as you play, and finally open it completely. These passages have an extraordinary effect if they are employed in the right place and in the most perfect manner.

Ex. 80

On the contrary, the *decrescendo* (representing, for example, the setting sun) can be interpreted extremely well. You begin the passage *fortissimo* with the lid open and without the dampers, allow the lid to fall little by little for the *piano* and end *pianissimo* with the dampers.

Ex. 81

In many short phrases, a fine effect can be created by raising the dampers midway through. It then resembles a rocket being launched or represents a person who angrily seizes another by the hand. In the following example, the abbreviation 'o' indicates that you play without the dampers and 'm' with the dampers.

Ex. 82

The harmonica can effectively be imitated without the dampers, but as with any instrument that you wish to imitate, you must treat it according to its true character. In general, the harmonica requires slow, tender pieces with sustained and resonant notes. To produce this sustaining power on the piano, however, there is no way other than the fast repetition of the one note, or the fast vibration of the hammer against the string as I have previously explained. All notes of both melody and accompaniment must in this case belong to the same chord, and when the chord changes, its notes, if the expression so permits, must be allowed to fade little by little or be damped, and the notes of the next chord begin immediately without the dampers. Without this precaution, the resonance of earlier notes and the sound of newly-played ones would produce an awful cacophony. When several notes are played many times one after another at a very fast tempo, you should put in various *crescendos* and *diminuendos* with the aid of the lid to imitate the rising and falling sound of bells. The melody, whether it be in the treble or the bass, should as far as possible be brought out clearly, and runs and chromatic passages in particular should be avoided or, *when they occur*, played with the dampers. You should make frequent use of the piano lid since a great deal depends on that, though clearly this requires a lot of practice. It is gradually raised, for example, to swell a long-held note and allowed to fall just as slowly to decrease the tone. The bass line of such pieces should consist of few notes which, however, are struck a little more strongly. [In the following example], particular attention should be paid to the *piano* and *forte*, and to the marking < > which represents the raising and lowering of the lid.

Ex. 83

The leather register without the dampers is also a very beautiful mutation. With this, you can imitate the music of a Spanish character in which round, wooden plates of various sizes, tuned to definite pitches, are struck. To mimic music of this kind as strikingly as possible, both hands must play *mezzo forte* in the treble clef with the lid closed.

Ex. 84

Using the leather register without the dampers and with the lid open the left hand part can very effectively imitate the tambourine.

Ex. 85

Also, using the leather stop without the dampers, you can provide a very close imitation of the harp if the keyboard writing adopts the character of the instrument.

Ex. 86

To imitate the mandolin, you must perform on the piano in the following way, without pedal and with the lid closed.

Ex. 87

The mutation that causes the hammer to strike only one string sounds very well and, when played with the lid closed, represents distant music or the answer of an echo. Players who possess [real] musical feeling, will use it frequently, for example, for various [tonal] variations in an arietta, where a *pianissimo* can be played with the lid closed and with one string, and the following fortissimo with the lid raised and with both strings, which produces a very beautiful contrast. I do not really like using this pedal for *crescendos* and *diminuendos*; the sudden change of tone quality [created] by the second string makes the transition too perceptible.

Ex. 88

Every conceivable kind of musical expression can undoubtedly be achieved by means of the lid if you know how to use it with skill; in particular, such markings as > < <> >< can be expressed extraordinarily well, and for certain notes of long duration, you can strengthen the sound of a note already played by raising the lid. See the following examples.

Ex. 89   Ex. 90   Ex. 91

To end this chapter, I must observe furthermore that it is always better to play the piano with the lid closed so that the movement of the hammers and entire mechanism is less audible. You also have the advantage in this way of being able to produce a *forte* or *fortissimo* effectively by raising the lid. Nevertheless, as I have already mentioned on p. 52, beginners should take all possible care to express the full range of musical dynamics with their fingers [alone] and only then, when they have mastered this expressive finger touch, may they use the lid and the other mutations, and thereby impart consummate expressivity to their playing. Clearly, much skill is needed to be able to use all the mutations described in this chapter effectively and to be able to assign each one to its proper place; also, a very fine instrument is required. If any readers of my book should wish to possess a piano of this kind, they can come to me with complete confidence; I promise that they will receive absolute satisfaction. My reputation and my honour are laid down in this respect, for I will always stand for my pledge as an artist and honest man.

Louis Adam, *Méthode de piano du Conservatoire* (Paris 1804)

Chapter 10 (pp. 218–23)
The manner of using the pedals

Nothing on an instrument that adds to the charm of the music, and the emotions, should be neglected, and in this respect the pedals used appropriately and skilfully obtain very great benefits.

The pianoforte can only prolong the sound of a note for the duration of a bar and the sound diminishes so rapidly that the ear has difficulty in grasping and understanding it. Since the pedals remedy this defect and serve at the same time to prolong a sound with equal force for several bars at a time, it would be quite wrong to renounce their use. We know that some people, by a blind attachment to the old rules, by a proper but badly understood affection, forbid their use and call it charlatanism. We will be of their opinion when they make this objection against those performers who only use the pedals to dazzle the ignorant in music, or to disguise the mediocrity of their talent; but those who only use them appropriately to enhance and sustain the sounds of a beautiful melody and fine harmony assuredly merit the approval of true connoisseurs.

Since several composers have written music especially for the use of the pedals, we will first of all acquaint students with their mechanism, and then the manner of their use.

On ordinary small pianos there are only two pedals placed to the left. The one on the outside damps the sounds even more than usual, and one commonly calls it: *jeu de Luth* [lute] or *jeu de Harpe* [harp]; it only produces dry and very damped sounds. The second serves to raise the dampers (it is also known by the name *grande pédale*,) and allows all the strings to vibrate indistinctly. There are also larger square pianos with four pedals. The pedals are placed in the middle of the instrument. The first two which are on the outside are the same as those of the small piano; the third is the pedal that one calls *jeu céleste* [moderator], and the almost useless fourth only serves to raise the lid of the piano.*

Grand pianos, in the form of a harpsichord, also have four pedals; but each one serves a useful purpose.

* Nb. On large English square pianos there are only three pedals and no *jeu céleste*; the third does the job of our fourth, that is to say it raises the lid.

The first three are the same as those of square pianos; it is only the fourth one which differs and which can only be adapted to grand pianos.

This fourth pedal makes the keyboard move towards the right, gradually removing the hammers from the strings, until only one [string] remains over the hammer, and it is with this pedal that one achieves a perfect *pianissimo*.

On English pianos of this type, this last pedal is normally placed at the extreme left. The sustaining pedal is placed at the extreme right; the others are sometimes found under the instrument to be pushed by the knees.

Many people think that the sustaining pedal is only used to make a *forte*, but they are mistaken; this pedal which allows the strings to vibrate indistinctly only produces a confusion of sounds disagreeable to the ear[.] We will now show how it is used.

The sustaining pedal must only be used in [passages of] consonant chords, where the melody is very slow and the harmony never changes; if these chords are followed by another which no longer agrees or which changes the harmony, it is necessary to damp the preceding chord and re-take the pedal on the following chord, having care always to raise it before each chord of which the harmony is not to be the same as the preceding.

In general one should only use this pedal to make a *forte* in slow movements, and when it is necessary to sustain the same bass or the same melody note for several bars without interruption or modulation. One easily notices that if the pedal is applied to a melody which is quick, or full of scales, the sounds mingle in such a manner that one cannot any longer distinguish the melody. Nothing produces a worse effect than when one plays chromatic scales with this pedal in a fast movement, or scales in thirds. It is however the greatest resource of mediocre talents.

One proof of particularly bad taste is the use of this pedal indistinctly for all passages; as one is sure of producing good effects with it appropriately, so one can be sure to displease and to tire by employing it in a contrary manner.

This pedal is a good deal more agreeable when one uses it to express gentleness, but it is necessary to have care in attacking the keys with great delicacy and in a softer manner than if one played without pedal. The sound of the instrument is naturally louder when the dampers are raised, and a single note makes all the others vibrate at the same time if one presses with too much force, something which never happens when one strikes the key gently.

This pedal and manner of playing quietly should only be used for pure, harmonious melodies whose sounds can be held for a long time, as for example in pastorales and musettes, tender and melancholy airs, romances, religious pieces and in general in all expressive passages where the melodies are very slow and only rarely change harmony.

The first pedal which is at the end of the piano and which one calls *jeu de Luth ou de Harpe* [lute or harp] should only be used in fast passages: in *staccatos* for arpeggiated variations, and rapid chromatic scales, and all those places in general where the notes should be played distinctly.

This pedal, by the dryness that it gives to the sounds, adds greatly to the clarity of a passage and renders it very brilliant, but also, if one misses a single note, one notices it easily since none of the very dry, detached notes can escape the ear.

When the right hand plays arpeggios at speed, or detached notes, while sustained notes are found in the left, one may then add to that pedal the one which raises the dampers, which takes away the dryness of the sounds in the bass, by giving some vibration to the strings that one wants to sustain.

One can also use this pedal for accompanying the voice in those places where one needs to imitate the *staccato* or *pizzicato* of stringed instruments.

The third pedal, called *jeu céleste*, should only be used alone to express a piano, the sound becoming much weaker than in ordinary performance on the piano without pedal.

This pedal is only really *celestial* when one adds it to the second. It should only be used to play quietly and the sustaining pedal should be quit at each rest that is encountered and each change of harmony to avoid confusion of the sounds; it is in this manner that one succeeds perfectly in imitating the harmonica, whose tones act so powerfully on our feelings, and also in multiplying these effects by a considerable extension of the bass register which the harmonica does not possess.

The two pedals together make the sustaining of chords by means of the *Tremando* work very well; but *Tremando* must not be misunderstood to mean the movement of the fingers that one uses to touch alternately one note after another: the *Tremando* must be made with sufficient speed so that the sounds only present a continuity of sound to the ear.

To succeed in executing it it is necessary that the fingers never leave the keys, and that the strings are made to vibrate without interruption of the sound by a small quivering [of the fingers], particularly in the *diminuendo* and *pianissimo*, where the sounds must die away in such a manner that no movement of the keys is heard.

The fourth pedal of grand pianos in the form of a harpsichord should only be used to make the *piano*, *crescendo* and *diminuendo*. One can almost make the same effects on a grand piano with the fourth as with the second pedal, and on square pianos with four pedals, with the third and second, by using them, as we have already observed, for harmonious and sustained melodies, where the sounds do not mingle with one another.

(*Note.*) Up to the present the signs for the use of the pedals have still not been fixed.

Some mark them by the word 'pédale' and put any sort of sign in the place where they should be quit; others employ the sign ⊖ for the first pedal, ⊖ for the second and ⊜ for the third and when one needs to release them they mark them by the signs ⊕ ⊕ ⊕.

One could adopt a much simpler way which is to put 'pe' in the place where the pedals should be used, and put 𝄽ᵉ for the first pedal, 𝄽ᵉ for the second and 𝄽ᵉ for the third; in the place where the pedals should be released one could put a zero underneath the pedal which would be for the first pedal 𝄽ᵉ , for the second 𝄽ᵉ , and for the third 𝄽ᵉ .

[Six pages of examples from Adam's own works follow.]

Daniel Steibelt, *Méthode de piano* (Paris and Leipzig 1809)

[The text appeared simultaneously in French and German. The following translation is based on the German text.]

[Page 2] A sure art of striking the keys and of bending the fingers, a truly characteristic use of the registers (Züge) (mutations of tone by means of the pedal), otherwise little used and of which I was the first to demonstrate the advantages, gives the instrument a quite different expression. To begin with this use of the registers was described as charlatanism, and students disliked them; but those who outlawed them are overcoming their prejudice, while at the same time many of them do not yet know how to use these registers skilfully.

In the following I will show how this important addition to the instrument serves to bring out the colours better and to give light and shade to the performance, and that their use is subject to the rules of good taste.

[Pages 64 – 5]   Of the piano's registers (Zügen)
              Of the art of their use and their indication

The newest pianos have four registers, that is, tone mutations, brought into play by levers (by means of the knee on many pianos). Each of these registers has a particular sign in the music by which its use is indicated.

The first, which is known as the Piano, Muffle, or Lute register and is indicated with ⌘, damps the sounds even more than when no register is used. It must not be used alone, but always in conjunction with the following, which is moreover worked by the same foot. The combination of both these registers produces a tone which is similar to that of the harp or lute.

The second register, indicated by ⊕, raises the dampers which rest on each string. When one uses this register, the strings (which are struck by the hammers, by means of the keys) continue to vibrate as long as they are able; if the foot is removed, they are damped. This sustaining of the strings can last for two bars in an Adagio.

Ex. 92

The pedal must be used with understanding and care, and never in runs or fast passages. It is suitable for melodic movements which do not go too low. It can also be used when the left hand has particular passages such as the following:

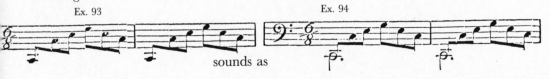

Ex. 93   sounds as   Ex. 94

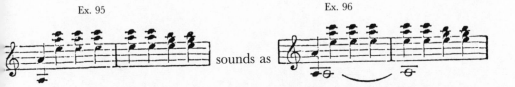

Ex. 95   sounds as   Ex. 96

The third register, indicated by ⊞ , is the bassoon register. If it is to make the proper effect, it must never be used without the second register. The use of this register requires great care and judgement. It is necessary to remark that if it is used alone the tone of the instrument becomes harsh. One must also take care to release the second pedal a little earlier than the third.

The fourth register, indicated by ↑ , causes one string to be struck, and is also known as the Pianissimo; it slides the keyboard in such a manner that the hammer, which previously struck three strings, now only hits one.

A delightful effect is produced when the three last registers are used together in slow, full-toned pieces without modulation.

Those register signs which were taken up by Clementi, Dussek and Cramer were first invented by us.

The sign * placed over one of the register signs signifies that the foot must be raised and the register released. It has a similar effect to a natural sign ♮ placed before a note sharpened by a ♯. If two or more register signs are combined, the registers which are indicated should be taken together, e.g.

⊕ or ⊞ and so forth, and when the release sign * stands next to one of two register signs combined together, the register that is indicated should be released, but the other held until it is likewise taken of by a *.

If only a single register has been taken, the release sign alone is used when it should be taken off.

Notes

Introduction

1 Obviously, the construction of the early piano is important in this context, particularly the differences between 'English' and 'Viennese' actions. Precise descriptions of each can be found in all major texts on the history of the piano. See, for example, R. Harding, *The Piano-Forte* (Old Woking 2/1978).

1 The transition from the harpsichord and clavichord to the piano

1 G. Montanari, Bartolomeo Cristofori', *EM* 19 (1991), pp. 385–96.
2 Scipione Maffei, 'Nuova Invenzione d'un Gravecembalo col piano, e forte . . .', *Giornale de' Litterati d'Italia* 5, p. 144 (Venice 1711), translated in Harding, *The Piano-Forte*, pp. 5–6.
3 Described in S. Pollens, 'The Pianos of Bartolomeo Cristofori', *JAMIS* (1984), pp. 32–68.
4 *Ibid* and S. Pollens, 'The Early Portuguese Piano', *EM* 13 (1985), pp. 18–27. See also S. Pollens, 'Three Keyboard Instruments Signed by Cristofori's Assistant, Giovanni Ferrini', *GSJ* 44 (1991), pp. 77–93; L. Tagliavini, 'Giovanni Ferrini and his Harpsichord "a penne e a martelletti"', *EM* 19 (1991), pp. 399–408; S. Pollens, 'An Upright Pianoforte by Domenico del Mela', *GSJ* 45 (1992), pp. 22–8.
5 E Badura-Skoda, 'Zur Fruhgeschichte des Hammerklaviers' in *Festschrift H. Federhofer* (Tutzing 1988), pp 37–44.
6 His actions of c.1720 are discussed in L. Mizler, *Neue eröffnete musikalische Bibliothek* (4 vols., Leipzig 1747), vol. III, pp. 474–7.
7 J. Adlung, *Musica Mechanica Organoedi* (2 vols., Berlin 1768) vol. II, pp. 115–17.
8 S. Pollens, 'Gottfried Silbermann's pianos', *Organ Yearbook* 17 (1986), pp. 103–21.
9 Letter of William Mason to Thomas Gray, 27 June 1755. See *The Correspondence of Thomas Gray*, ed. P. Toynbee and L Whibley (Oxford 1971).
10 T. Mortimer, *Universal Director* (London 1763), 50.
11 See R. Maunder, 'The Earliest English Square Piano', *GSJ* 42 (1989), pp. 77–84.
12 E. de Bricqueville, *Les Ventes d'instruments de musique au XVIIIᵉ siècle* (Paris 1908), p. 11.
13 *L'Avant Coureur*, April 1761.
14 See Pollens, 'The Pianos of Bartolomeo Cristofori'.
15 Translation in R. Russell, *The Harpsichord and Clavichord* (London 2/1973), p. 185.
16 C. Burney, *The Present State of Music in France and Italy* (London 1771; ed. P. Scholes, London 1959), Scholes edn, p. 152.
17 Agricola supplied much information to Adlung for his 1768 publication.
18 *Spenersche Zeitung* 11 May 1747, translated in C. Wolff, 'New Research on Bach's *Musical Offering*', *MQ* 57 (1971), p. 401.

19 See Wolff, 'New Research', p. 401.

20 *Ibid.*, p. 403.

21 E. Badura-Skoda, 'Prologomena to a History of the Viennese Forte-Piano', *Israel Studies in Musicology* 2 (1980), p. 77.

22 E. Rimbault, *The Pianoforte* (London 1924), p. 5, and the *Public Advertiser*, 2 June 1768. J. C. Bach's op. 5 sonatas 'for Piano Forte or Harpsichord' were advertised in the *Public Advertiser* on 17 April 1766.

23 *Mercure de France* 1 October 1768, p. 149.

24 W. H. Cole, 'Americus Backers: Original Forte Piano Maker', *The Harpsichord and Pianoforte Magazine* 4 (1987), pp 79–85.

25 The earliest extant piano made in France is a square piano by Mercken dated 1770.

26 This 'harpsichord with hammers' is mentioned in an inventory of Blanchet's workshop quoted in F. Hubbard, *Three Centuries of Harpsichord Making* (Cambridge, Mass. 1965), p. 293.

27 Burney, *Present State of Music in France and Italy*, Scholes edn, p. 27.

28 D. Diderot, *Correspondance* ed. G. Roth (16 vols., Paris 1955–70), vol. XI, pp. 197, 213 (letters of 26 September and 28 October 1771).

29 See Chapter 3, note 18 (p. 32).

30 *Journal de Musique* 5 (Paris 1773), p. 16.

31 See J. Gallay, *Un Inventaire sous la Terreur. Etat des instruments de musique relevés chez les émigrés et condamnés par H. Bruni* (Paris 1890).

32 E. Closson, 'Pascal Taskin', *Sammelbande der Internationalen Musikgesellschaft* (1910–11), pp. 234–67.

33 Hubbard, *Three Centuries*, pp. 295–8.

34 *Ibid.*, pp. 310–12.

35 *Erard. Du clavecin méchanique au piano en forme de clavecin.* Catalogue of exhibition at the Conservatoire National Supérieur de Musique, Paris, June–November 1979, p. 11.

36 C. Burney, *The Present State of Music in Germany, the Netherlands and United Provinces* (London 1773; ed. P. Scholes, London 1959), Scholes edn, p. 39.

37 *Ibid.*, p. 96.

38 *Ibid.*, p. 160.

39 See notes 7 and 17 above.

40 Adlung, *Musica Mechanica Organoedi*, vol. II, p. 117.

41 See note 18 above.

42 Burney, *Present State of Music in Germany*, Scholes edn, pp. 200–1.

43 The inventory was published as the *Verzeichniss des musikalischen Nachlass des verstorbenen Capellmeisters Carl Phillipp Emmanuel Bach* (Hamburg 1790; facsmile edn by R. Wade, New York and London 1981).

44 See, for example, J. F. Reichardt's description in his *Briefe eines aufmerksamen Reisenden die Musik betreffend* (2 vols., Frankfurt and Leipzig 1774–6), vol. II, p. 16.

45 J. Mattheson, *Critica Musica* (2 vols., Hamburg 1725), vol II, p. 340.

46 See note 9 above.

47 J. Sittard, *Geschichte des Musik- und Concertwesens in Hamburg* (Stuttgart 1890), p. 182.

48 J. A. Hiller, *Wöchentliche Nachrichten und Anmerkungen die Musik betreffend* (Leipzig, 24 July 1769).

49 See Voltaire's letter of c.15 December 1774 in *The Complete Works of Voltaire* (The Voltaire Foundation, vol. CXXV, Banbury 1975).

50 C. Pierre, *Histoire du Concert Spirituel 1725–1790* (Paris 1975).

51 Performances by Hook, Clementi and others are mentioned in the contemporary London press.

52 For an assessment of Mozart's keyboard instruments see R. Maunder, 'Mozart's Keyboard Instruments', *EM* 20 (1992), pp. 207–19.

2 Stops, levers and pedals

1 F. Couperin, *Pieces de Clavecin . . . Premier Livre* (Paris 1713), Preface.

2 Thomas Mace, *Musick's Monument* (London 1676), pp. 235–6.

3 See E. Ripin, 'Expressive Devices Applied to the Eighteenth-Century Harpsichord', *Organ Yearbook* 1 (1970), pp. 64–80.

4 For a full description of the device see Ripin, 'Expressive Devices'.

5 *Ibid.*

6 *Histoire de l'Académie Royale des Sciences* (Paris 1765), p. 242.

7 S. Marcuse, *A Survey of Musical Instruments* (London 1975), pp. 274–5.

8 Abbé Trouflaut, 'Lettre aux auteurs de ce journal', *Journal de Musique* 5 (Paris, 1773), p. 10.

9 D. Boalch, *Makers of the Harpsichord and Clavichord* (London 2/1974), s.v. "Erard".

10 G. Kinsky, *Katalog des Musikhistorisches Museum von Wilhelm Heyer in Köln* (2 vols., Cologne 1912), vol II, p. 671.

11 *Magazin der Musik* (Hamburg, 1783), p. 1025.

12 Boalch, *Makers*, s.v. 'Prosperi'.

13 Russell, *The Harpsichord and Clavichord*, p. 15.

14 Pollens, 'The Pianos of Bartolomeo Cristofori'.

15 Pollens, 'The Early Portuguese Piano'.

16 Pollens, 'Gottfried Silbermann's Pianos'.

17 *Ibid.*, p. 106.

18 See the Friederici piano dated 1745 in the Conservatoire Museum, Brussels.

19 Walter grand, c.1778, now in the Rück collection: Mozart's piano in the Internationale Stiftung Mozarteum, Salzburg.

20 A Walter grand, c.1785, now in the Kunsthistorisches Museum, Vienna, has a third lever operating the bassoon.

21 An enthusiastic account of Walter's pianos is given in the *Jahrbuch der Tonkunst von Wien und Prag* (Prague 1796, R/1975), pp. 87–91.

22 See note 7 above.

23 An account of the extant pianos by Graf is given in Deborah Wythe's article 'The Pianos of Conrad Graf', *EM* 12 (1984), pp. 447–60.

24 *Ibid.*, p. 457.

25 B. Brauchli, 'Christian Baumann's Square Pianos and Mozart', *GSJ* 45 (1992), pp. 29–49.

26 K. Mobbs, 'Stops and Other Special Effects on the Early Piano', *EM* 12 (1984), p. 472.

27 Mr C. F. Colt brought this instrument to my notice.

28 It is described in detail in Mobbs, 'Stops and Other Special Effects', pp. 474–5.

29 Maunder, 'The Earliest English Square Piano', p. 81.

30 *Descriptions des machines et procédés* (Paris 1811–63, old series), no. 11754.

31 *Rapports du jury* from the 1855 Paris Exhibition (Paris 1856), p. 46.

32 *Ibid.*

33 *Reports of the Juries* from the 1862 London Exhibition (London 1863), pp. 6–7.

34 *Rapports du jury*, pp. 46–7.

35 *Ibid.*

36 H. Schmitt, *Das Pedal des Clavieres* (Vienna 1875; Eng trans. Philidelphia 1893), trans., p. 82.

37 G. Grove, ed., *A Dictionary of Music and Musicians* (London 1879–89), s.v. 'Pedals'.

38 Schmitt, *Das Pedal*, trans., p. 82.

39 J. Broadwood & Co., *Pianofortes* (London 1892), p. 32.

40 Personal communication from the firm.

41 Personal communication from the firm.

3 Documentary accounts of early pedalling

1 J. P. Milchmeyer, *Die wahre Art das Pianoforte zu spielen* (Dresden 1797), p. 58.
2 L. Adam, *Méthode de piano du Conservatoire* (Paris 1804), p. 218.
3 D. Steibelt, *Méthode de piano* (Paris and Leipzig 1809), p.2.
4 F.-J. Fetis, 'Improvements in the Construction of Pianos', *Harmonicon* 5 (1827), p. 158.
5 Pollens, 'Gottfried Silbermann's Pianos', pp. 102–21. A similar device was patented in 1788 by Samuel Bury: see Harding, *The Piano-Forte*, p. 341.
6 Mattheson, *Critica Musica*, vol. II, p. 248; translated in A. Loesser, *Men, Women and Pianos* (New York 1954), pp. 26–7.
7 Hebenstreit's pupils included Kuhnau, J. C. Richter, C. S. Binder, G. Gebel, M. Hellmann, Grumpenhuber and Noelli: see S. E. Hanks, 'Pantaleon's Pantalon: an Eighteenth-Century Musical Fashion', *MQ* 55 (1969), p. 215.
8 Mizler, *Neue eröffnete musikalische Bibliothek*, vol. III, p. 474.
9 J. Beckmann, *Beiträge zur Geschichte der Erfindungen* (5 vols., Leipzig 1783–6, R/1965), vol I, p. 502 (trans. London 1817), trans., vol. III, p. 510.
10 *Ibid.* Mozart commented on this issue in his famous letter about Stein's pianos of 17 October 1777, as did Forkel in his *Musikalischer Almanach für Deutschland* (Leipzig 1783), p. 16.
11 Samuel Bury's patent quoted in Harding, *The Piano-Forte*, p. 341.
12 Dom Bédos de Celles, *L'Art du facteur d'orgues* (4 vols., Paris 1766–78, R/1963–6), vol. IV, p. 635.
13 F. H. J. Castil-Blaze, *Dictionnaire de Musique Moderne* (Paris 1821), s.v. 'Timpanon'.
14 N. Streicher, *Kurze Bemerkungen über das Spielen, Stimmen und Erhalten der Fortepiano* (Vienna 1801; trans. Ann Arbor 1983), trans., p. 5.
15 J. Adlung, *Anleitung zu der musikalischen Gelahrheit* (Erfurt 1758, R/1953), p. 560.
16 Hiller, *Wöchentliche Nachrichten* (24 July 1766), p. 32.
17 C. P. E. Bach, *Versuch über die wahre Art das Clavier zu spielen* (Berlin 1753–62; Eng. trans. London 1974), trans, p. 431.
18 C. Burney, *Music, Men and Manners in France and Italy*, ed. H. E. Poole (London 2/1974), pp. 19–20.
19 Adlung, *Anleitung*, p. 560.
20 E. Closson, *Histoire du piano* (Brussels 1944; Eng. trans. London 1947, 2/1974), trans., pp. 71–2; my italics.
21 D. G. Türk, *Klavierschule* (Leipzig 1789), p. 12.
22 W. Dale, *Tschudi, the Harpsichord Maker* (London 1913), p. 2.
23 Q. van Blankenburg, *Elementa Musica* ('s-Gravenhage, 1739), translated in Ripin, 'Expressive Devices', p. 64.
24 F.-J. Fétis, 'Memoir of Erard', *Harmonicon* 9 (1831), p. 256.
25 Cramer's *Magazin der Musik* (1783), pp. 1024–8.
26 J. S. Petri, *Anleitung zur practischen Musik* (Lauben 1767), p. 332.
27 Reichardt, *Briefe eines aufmerksamen Reisenden*, vol. II, p. 18.
28 N. E. Framery and P. L. Ginguené, *Encyclopédie méthodique: musique* (Paris 1791–1818), p. 287; trans. Hubbard in *Three Centuries*, p. 254.
29 F. C. Morse, *Furniture of the Olden Time* (New York 1902), pp. 261–2.
30 F. Kalkbrenner, *Méthode pour apprendre le pianoforte* (Paris 1830; Eng. trans. London 1862), trans, p. 10.
31 Ripin, 'Expressive Devices', p. 70.
32 See note 1 above.
33 Milchmeyer, *Die wahre Art*, p. 58.
34 J. H. Rieger, *Méthode analitique pour l'étude de pianoforte* (Paris 1820), p. 284.
35 C. Chaulieu, 'Des pédales du piano', *Le Pianiste* 9 (1833–4), p. 131.

36 F.-J. Fétis, *Biographie universelle* (Paris 1865), s.v. 'Steibelt'.

37 F. W. Wegeler and F. Ries, *Biographische Notizen über Ludwig van Beethoven* (Koblenz 1838, 2/1906), translated in A. W. Thayer, *The Life of Ludwig van Beethoven* (2 vols., London 1921), vol. I, p. 268.

38 A. Simpson and S. Horsfall, 'A Czech Composer Views His Comtemporaries: Extracts from the Memoirs of Tomasek; *MT* 115 (1974), p. 287.

39 Adam, *Méthode*, p. 218.

40 Chaulieu, '*Des pédales*', p. 131.

41 *AMZ* 11 (1809), pp. 601–3; translated in H. A. Craw, 'A Biography and Thematic Catalog of the Works of J. L. Dussek' (Ph.D. dissertation, University of Southern California 1964), p. 172.

42 *Le Pianiste* 6 (1864), p. 83.

43 Steibelt, *Méthode*, p. 2.

44 Ripin, 'Expressive Devices', p. 66.

45 *Encyclopaedia Britannica* (London 3/1801), s.v. 'Pianoforte'.

46 Kalkbrenner, *Méthode*, trans., p. 10.

47 C. Czerny, *Vollständige theoretisch-practische Pianoforteschule* op. 500 (3 vols., Vienna 1838–9; Eng. trans. London 1838–9), trans., vol. II, p. 100.

48 *Ibid.*, vol. III, pp. 62–4.

49 E. Anderson, ed., *The Letters of Mozart and his Family* (London 3/1985), p. 793.

50 *Caecilia* 10 (1829), pp. 238–9.

51 *Ibid.*

52 W. Nicholson, *The British Encyclopaedia* (London 1809) s.v. 'Musical Instruments'.

53 See note 30 above.

54 *AMZ* 1 (1798–9), p. 136.

55 *AMZ* 4 (1801–2), p. 226.

56 C. Czerny, 'Erinnerungen aus meinem Leben' (MS 1842); Eng. trans. in *MQ* 42 (1956), p. 309.

57 J. N. Hummel, *Ausführliche, theoretisch-practische Anweisung zum Pianoforte-Spiele* (3 vols., Vienna 1828; Eng. trans. London 1828), trans., vol. III, p. 62.

58 *Ibid.*

59 in his *Trois Amusements* op. 105 no. 1. (1824).

60 Czerny, op. 500, trans., vol. III, p. 64.

61 See note 30 above.

62 Quoted in C. Flamm, 'Ein Verlegerbriefwechsel zur Beethovenzeit' in *Beethoven-Studien* (Vienna, 1970) p. 75.

4 Early techniques of the pedals as described in tutors

1 C. P. E. Bach, *Versuch*, trans., p. 431.

2 Some Broadwood grands up to c.1810 had Venetian swells, but the device (or an equivalent) was not used on 'Viennese' pianos. I am indebted to David Hunt for this information.

3 Czerny, op. 500, trans., vol. III, p. 61.

4 A more extensive discussion of the development of this figuration can be found in my chapter 'The Nocturne: Development of a New Style' in J. Samson, ed., *The Cambridge Companion to Chopin* (Cambridge 1992), pp. 32–49.

5 J. B. Cramer, *Instructions for the Pianoforte* (London 1812, 3/1818), 1818 edn, p. 43.

6 Hummel, *Anweisung zum Pianoforte-Spiele*, trans., vol. III, p. 62.

7 Kalkbrenner, *Méthode*, trans., p. 10.

8 J. Jousse, *The Pianoforte Made Easy* (London 5/c. 1820), p. 37.

9 J. Monro, *A New and Complete Introduction to the Art of Playing on the Pianoforte* (London 1820), p. 46.

10 C. P. E. Bach, *Versuch*, trans., p. 150.

11 Kalkbrenner, *Méthode*, trans., p. 12; and Czerny, op. 500, trans., vol. III, pp. 55–6.

12 K. Engel, *The Pianist's Handbook* (London 1853), p. 64.

13 C. P. E. Bach, *Versuch*, trans., p. 155.

14 Adam, *Méthode*, pp. 151–2.

15 I. Moscheles, *Studies for the Pianoforte op. 70* (London 1827), p. 3.

16 Engel, *The Pianist's Handbook*, p. 64.

17 A. Bertini, *New System for Learning and Acquiring Extraordinary Facility on all Musical Instruments, Particularly the Pianoforte* (London 1830), p. 5.

18 Adam, *Méthode*, p. 84.

19 M. Clementi, *Appendix to the Fifth Edition of Clementi's Introduction* (London 1811), p. 4.

20 Kalkbrenner, *Méthode*, trans., p. 55.

5 Early pedal markings

1 C. Czerny, *Supplement (oder vierter Theil) zur grossen Pianoforte Schule* (Vienna 1846–7; Eng. trans. London 1846–7), trans., p 2.

2 For questions of dating, see B. Cooper, 'The Ink in Beethoven's "Kafka" Sketch Miscellany', *ML* 68 (1987), pp 315–32.

3 Quoted in G. Müller, *Daniel Steibelt* (Leipzig 1933), p. 92.

4 A. Méreaux, *Les Clavecinistes de 1637 à 1790* (Paris 1867), p. 81; F.-J. Fétis, 'Etat actuel de la musique en France', *L'Europe Littéraire* 69 (1833), p. 277.

5 R. Gerig, *Famous Pianists and their Technique* (Newton Abbot 1976), p. 124.

6 H. Schonberg, *The Great Pianists* (London 1963), p. 68.

7 Kalkbrenner, *Méthode*, trans., p. 10.

8 A. Ringer, 'Beethoven and the London Pianoforte School', *MQ* 56 (1970), pp. 742–58.

9 W. Newman, 'Beethoven's Pianos Versus His Piano Ideals', *JAMS* 23 (1970), pp. 484–504.

10 See note 1 above.

11 *New Edition with Considerable Improvements of Sonata no. 2 from Opera II* (Clementi, Collard, Davis and Collard c.1818/19).

6 Mozart and his contemporaries

1 Anderson, ed., *The Letters of Mozart*, p. 329.

2 See Maunder, 'Mozart's Keyboard Instruments'.

3 While there are no pedalboards with completely independent actions in existence, three pedal pianos by the Salzburg maker Johann Schmid (1757–1804) survive. In these pianos various mechanisms (in one case including a separate set of strings) were constructed within the case of the piano itself. Further details can be found im *Saitenklaviere im Salzburger Museum Carolino Augusteum* (Salzburg 1988).

4 O. E. Deutsch, *Mozart: A Documentary Biography* (Eng. trans. London 1966), p. 239.

5 Anderson, ed., *The Letters of Mozart*, pp. 888–9.

6 Deutsch, *Mozart*, p. 237.

7 *Neue Mozart Ausgabe: Kritische Berichte*, series 5 workgroup 15, vol. VI (Basel, London and New York 1986), p. 25.

8 The idiosyncratic arrangement of organ pedalboards in Austria is described in P. Williams, *A New History of the Organ from the Greeks to the Present Day* (London 1980) and A. Forer, *Orgeln in Österreich* (Vienna and Munich 1973). Various short-octave arrangements were used, some of them very complex. Mozart wrote about Stein's organs in his letter of 17 October, 1777:

'At first the pedal seemed a bit strange to me, as it was not divided. It started with C, and then D and E followed in the same row. But with us D and E are above, as E♭ and F♯ are here', (Anderson, ed., *The Letters of Mozart*).

9 Deutsch, *Mozart*, pp. 325, 561.

10 *Ibid.*, p. 586.

11 See note 2 above.

12 *The Collected Works of Johann Christian Bach*, vol. XLII, ed. S. Roe (New York and London 1989), p. ix.

13 C. P. E. Bach, *Versuch*, trans., p. 431.

14 J. Sainsbury, *A Dictionary of Musicians* (London 1824), s.v. 'Noelli'.

15 H. Walter, 'Das Tasteninstrument beim jungen Haydn' in *Der junge Haydn: Internationalen Arbeitstagung des Instituts fur Aufführungspraxis* (Graz 1970), p. 237.

16 H. C. R. Landon, *Haydn: Chronicle and Works* (5 vols., London 1976–80), vol. III, p. 445.

17 T. Latour, *Sequel to Latour's Instructions for the Pianoforte* (London 1828), p. 2. See also Cramer, *Instructions*, p. 43 and other London tutors.

7 The emergence of modern pedalling

1 *The Pedals of the Piano-Forte*, trans. S. Law.

2 L. Köhler, *Der Klavier-Pedalzug, seine Natur und künstlerische Anwendung* (Berlin 1882).

3 These include Rubinstein (1896), Venino (1893), Nicholls (1902), Breithaupt (1906), Mathews (1906), Vergil (1912) and many later authors: see bibliography for details.

4 A. Rubinstein, *Leitfallen zum richtigen Gebrauch des Pianoforte-Pedals* (Leipzig 1896; Eng. trans. 1897), trans., preface. Rubinstein's remarks were echoed in an article, 'The Literature of the Pianoforte Pedal' ('At the head and front stands *The Pedals of the Pianoforte* by Hans Schmitt. No earnest student can afford to overlook this book'), *Musician* 8 (1903), p. 427.

5 A. Quidant, *L'Ame du piano* (Paris 1875).

6 C. Moscheles, *Aus Moscheles' Leben* (2 vols., Leipzig 1872; Eng. trans. London 1873), trans., vol. I, p. 247.

7 F. Wieck, *Clavier und Gesang* (Leipzig 1853; Eng. trans. Boston 1872), trans., pp. 59–60.

8 *Ibid.*, pp. 63–4.

9 C. E. and M. Hallé, eds., *Life and Letters of Sir Charles Hallé* (London 1896), p. 70.

10 A. Kullak, *Die Aesthetik des Klavierspiels* (Berlin 1861; Eng. trans. of 3rd edn. 1893), trans., p. 307.

11 K. Goldmark, *Notes from the Life of a Viennese Composer* (New York 1927), p. 134.

12 Czerny, op. 500, trans., vol. III, p. 64.

13 *Ibid.*, p. 100.

14 F.-J. Fétis and I. Moscheles, *Méthode des méthodes de piano* (Paris 1837; Eng. trans. London 1841), trans., p. 11.

15 J. C. Fillmore, *A History of Piano Music* (London 1885), pp. 194–5.

16 F. Niecks, *Frederick Chopin as a Man and Musician* (2 vols., London 1888), vol. II, p. 98.

17 F. Niecks, 'On the Use and Abuse of the Pedal', *Monthly Musical Record* 6 (1876), p. 183.

8 The sustaining pedal after c.1800

1 W. von Lenz, *Die grossen Pianoforte-Virtuosen unserer Zeit* (Berlin 1872; Eng. trans. London 1899), trans., p. 43.

2 See, for example, L. Plantinga, *Clementi: His Life and Music* (London 1977), p. 247.

3 Chaulieu, 'Des Pédales', p. 132.

4 Kalkbrenner, *Méthode*, trans., p. 10.

5 Chaulieu, 'Des Pédales', p. 132.

6 C. Gardeton, *Almanach de la musique pour l'an 1819* (Paris 1820), p. 261. The article from which this extract is taken was poorly translated in *Harmonicon* 9 (1823), p. 123.

7 Kalkbrenner, *Méthode*, trans., p. 10.

8 Czerny, op. 500, vol. III, trans., pp. 61–2.

9 S. Thalberg, *L'Art du chant appliqué au piano* (Paris 1853), p. 3 – presumably Thalberg had the sustaining pedal chiefly in mind here.

10 P. J. G. Zimmerman, *Méthode de piano* (2 vols., Mainz 1840), vol. II, p. 61.

11 A. Lavignac, *L'Ecole de la pédale* (Paris 1889), p. 79.

12 *Ibid.*, p. 68.

13 *Ibid.*, p. 193.

14 Weick, *Clavier und Gesang*, trans., p. 60.

15 Czerny, *Supplement*, trans., p. 29.

16 *Ibid.*, p. 2.

17 Grove, ed., *Dictionary*, s.v. 'Henselt'.

18 *Ibid.*

19 B. Litzmann, *Clara Schumann* (3 vols., Leipzig 1902–8, R/1970; Eng. trans. 2 vols., London 1913, R/1972), trans., vol. I, p. 149.

20 *Ibid.*, vol. II, p. 227.

21 This instruction is found at the bottom of the first page of Clara Schumann's *Quatre Pièces* op. 5. Similar remarks occur in other works by her.

22 The description comes from a second-hand account in a letter by Kozmian quoted in A. Hedley, *Chopin* (London 3/1974), p. 67.

23 Niecks, *Frederick Chopin*, vol. II, pp. 88–9.

24 I. Moscheles, Op. 70, Study no. 9.

25 T. Matthay, *Musical Interpretation* (Boston 1913), p. 131.

26 E. Hipkins, *How Chopin Played* (London 1937), p. 19.

27 For a detailed examination of this process see Rowland, 'The Nocturne'.

28 Czerny, *Supplement*.

29 W. Mason, *Memoirs of a Musical Life* (New York 1901), pp. 210–11.

30 C. Moscheles, *Aus Moscheles' Leben*, trans., vol. II, pp. 12–13.

31 Grove, ed., *Dictionary*, s.v. ' Pollini'.

32 Niecks, *Frederick Chopin*, vol. II, p. 98.

33 J. G. Huneker, *Franz Liszt* (New York 1911), pp. 285–7.

34 W. Kuhe, *My Musical Recollections* (London 1896), p. 24.

35 A. Marmontel, *L'Art classique et moderne du piano* (Paris 1876), p. 146.

36 A. Marmontel, *Les Pianistes célèbres* (Paris 1878), p. 166.

37 J. Huneker, ed., *Letters of James Gibbons Huneker* (London 1922), p. 228.

38 *Revue et Gazette Musicale* (9 April 1837), translated in A. Williams, *Portrait of Liszt* (Oxford 1990), p. 88.

39 A. Fay, *Music-Study in Germany* (Chicago 1880), p. 220.

40 C. E. and M. Hallé, eds., *Sir Charles Hallé*, p. 37.

41 *Ibid.*, p. 37.

42 Fay, *Music-Study*, p. 205.

43 *Ibid.*, p. 276.

44 A. Friedheim, *Life and Liszt* (New York 1961), p. 46.

45 Fay, *Music-Study*, pp. 176–7.

46 All these markings occur in the *Album d'un Voyageur*.

47 Niecks, *Frederick Chopin*, vol. II, p. 337.

48 Marmontel, *Les Pianistes célèbres*, pp. 4–5; translated in J.-J. Eigeldinger, *Chopin, Pianist and Teacher* (Cambridge 3/1986), p. 274.

49 J. Kleczynski, *The Works of Frederic Chopin and their Proper Interpretation* (Eng. trans. London 1882), p. 39.

50 A. Strelezki, *Personal Recollections of Chats with Liszt* (London 1887), p. 12.

51 Eigeldinger, *Chopin*, pp. 256–7.

52 A. Marontel, *Histoire du piano et de ses origines* (Paris 1885), pp. 256–7.

53 R. Koczalski, *Frédéric Chopin* (Cologne 1936), p. 13.

54 L. Aguettant, *La Musique de piano des origines à Ravel* (Paris 1954), p. 196.

55 *Ibid.*, p. 150.

56 Kleczynski, *The Works of Frederic Chopin*, p. 45.

57 See, for example, Eigeldinger, *Chopin*, Appendix II.

58 C. Lachmund, *Mein Leben mit Franz Liszt* (Eschwege 1970), p. 81; translated in Eigeldinger, *Chopin*, p. 83.

59 A. Lindo, *Pedalling in Pianoforte Music* (London 1922), p. 37.

60 Czerny, op. 500, vol. III, p. 100.

61 F. Busoni, 'On the Transcription of Bach's Organ Works for the Pianoforte', first appendix to vol. I of J. S. Bach's *The Well-Tempered Clavichord* (New York 1894), p. 176.

62 R. Riefling, *Piano Pedalling* (Oslo 1957; Eng. trans. London 1962), Chapter 9.

63 J. Banowetz, *The Pianist's Guide to Pedalling* (Bloomington 1985), Chapter 5.

64 *Ibid.*, p. 231.

65 Riefling, *Piano Pedalling*, trans., p. 22.

66 *Ibid.*, pp. 4–16 for an account of several suggestions.

67 Gerig, *Famous Pianists*, p. 323.

68 See note 47 above.

9 Other pedals from c.1800

1 Some confusion has surrounded these terms in the literature on the pianoforte. See, for example, Harding, *The Piano-Forte*, p. 71.

2 Starke distinguishes between the 'Pianozug' (moderator), 'Gitarrezug' (una corda) and 'Pianissimozug' (more extreme moderator) in his *Wiener Pianoforteschule* (Vienna 1819–20), pp. 16–17.

3 Milchmeyer, *Die wahre Art*; see the Appendix (p. 163, Ex. 74).

4 Madame la Comtesse de Montgeroult, *Cours complet pour l'enseignment du fortepiano* (Paris c.1820), p. 210.

5 Harding, *The Piano-Forte*, p. 344.

6 H. Herz, *Méthode complète de piano* (Mainz 1838; Eng. trans. London 1839), trans., p. 15.

7 Quoted in Landon, *Haydn*, vol. III, p. 415.

8 *The Letters of Beethoven*, trans. and ed. E. Anderson (London 1961), letter no. 66. Anderson mistranslates 'Zug' as 'tension', but Beethoven clearly has the una corda in mind, which he refers to as 'den Zug mit einer Saite'.

9 Czerny, *Supplement*, trans., p. 107.

10 Translation from Banowetz, *Pedalling*, p. 163.

11 See note 6 above.

12 Czerny, op. 500, trans., vol. III, p. 65.

13 Czerny, *Supplement*, trans., p. 6.

14 *Méthode pour pianoforte par Pleyel et Dussek* (Paris 1799).

15 Chaulieu, 'Des Pédales', p. 132.

16 *AMZ* 9 (1807), p. 744; trans. in Craw, 'J. L. Dussek', p. 141.

17 Cramer, *Instructions*, p. 43.

18 Related by Field's pupil Dubuk in H. Dessauer, *John Field, sein Leben und seine Werke* (Langensalza 1912), p. 44.

19 Nicholson, *The British Encyclopaedia*, s.v. 'Musical Instruments'.

20 Jousse, *The Pianoforte Made Easy*, p. 37.

21 W. Crotch, *Preludes for the Pianoforte* (London 1822).

22 J. F. Burrowes, *The Tutor's Assistant for the Pianoforte* (London 1834), p. 37.

23 J. Clarke, *Instructions for the Pianoforte* (London 1830), p. 29.

24 A. J. Hipkins, *A Description and History of the Pianoforte* (London 1896), p. 41.

25 Mobbs, 'Stops and Other Special Effects', note 10.

26 Zimmerman, *Méthode*, vol. II, p. 61.

27 Fétis and Moscheles, *Méthode des méthodes*, trans., p. 88.

28 Czerny op. 500, trans., vol. III, p. 65.

29 *Ibid.*, pp. 64–5.

30 Hummel, *Anweisung zum Pianoforte-Spiele*, trans., vol. III, p. 62.

31 Herz, *Méthode*, trans., p. 15.

32 Kalkbrenner, *Méthode*, trans., p. 10.

33 Wieck, *Clavier und Gesang*, trans., pp. 65–6.

34 *Ibid.*, p. 70.

35 *Ibid.*, p. 71.

36 J. A. Wade, *Handbook to the Pianoforte* (London 1844), p. 61.

37 Marmontel, *Les Pianistes célèbres*, p. 24.

38 *Ibid.*, p. 144.

39 Kuhe, *Musical Recollections*, p. 24.

40 Grove, ed., *Dictionary*, s.v. 'Sordino'.

41 Harding, *The Piano-Forte*, p. 128.

42 R. Hughes, *The Musical Guide* (New York 1903), s.v. 'Sordine'.

43 R. Breithaupt, 'Von den Pedalen', *Die Musik* 6 (1906), p. 146.

44 M. Honeggar, *Dictionnaire de la musique* (Paris 1976) s.v. 'Una Corda'.

45 *Selected Correspondence of Fryderyk Chopin*, ed. and trans. A. Hedley (London 1962), p. 76.

46 *Conseils aux jeunes pianistes* (Paris 1904), p. 39; trans. in Eigeldinger, *Chopin*, p. 57.

47 Aguettant, *La Musique de piano*, p. 196; trans. in Eigeldinger, *Chopin*, p. 58.

48 Marmontel, *Histoire du piano*, pp. 256–7; trans. in Eigeldinger, *Chopin*, p. 58.

49 Eigeldinger, *Chopin*, pp. 206, 221.

50 Litzmann, *Clara Schumann*, trans., vol. II, p. 227.

51 *Ibid.*, p. 26.

52 Schmitt, *Das Pedal*, trans., p. 84.

53 *Ibid.*, p. 84.

54 *Ibid.*, p. 85.

55 Y. Bowen, *Pedalling the Modern Pianoforte* (London 1936), p. 27.

56 Schmitt, *Das Pedal*, trans., p. 82.

57 Liszt's letter is reproduced in facsimile in F. J. Hirt, *Meisterwerke des Klavierbaues* (Olten 1955; Eng. trans. London 1968), pp. 79–80.

58 Grove, ed., *Dictionary*, s.v. 'Pedals'.

59 Banowetz, *Pedalling*, pp. 90ff.

60 This occurs in the first of his *Trois Amusements* op. 105 (1824).

61 Fétis, 'Improvements', p. 158.

62 Hummel, *Anweisung zum Pianoforte-Spiele*, trans., vol. III, p. 62.

63 Czerny, op. 500, trans., vol. III, p. 65.

64 Schmitt, *Das Pedal*, trans., p. 85.

Select bibliography

Adam, L. *Méthode de piano du Conservatoire*. Paris 1804.

Adlung, J. *Anleitung zu der musikalischen Gelahrheit*. Erfurt 1758.

Musica Mechanica Organoedi. 2 vols., Berlin 1768.

Anderson, E., ed. *The Letters of Mozart and his Family*. London 3/1985.

Bach, C. P. E. *Versuch über die wahre Art das Clavier zu spielen*. Berlin 1753–62; Eng. trans. London 1974.

Badura-Skoda, E. 'Prologomena to a History of the Viennese Fortepiano'. *Israel Studies in Musicology* 2 (1980), pp. 77–99.

'Zur Frühgeschichte des Hammerklaviers' in *Festschrift H. Federhofer*. Tutzing 1988, pp. 37–44.

Banowetz, J. *The Pianist's Guide to Pedalling*. Bloomington 1985.

Bertini, A. *New Systems for Learning and Acquiring Extraordinary Facility on all Musical Instruments, Particularly the Pianoforte*. London 1830.

Boalch, D. *Makers of the Harpsichord and Clavichord*. London 2/1974.

Bontoft F. S. 'A Plea for "Una Corda"'. *The Musical Standard* 9 (1917), p. 60.

Brauchli, B. 'Christian Baumann's Square Pianos and Mozart'. *GSJ* 45 (1992), pp. 29–49.

Breithaupt, R. 'Von den Pedalen'. *Die Musik* 6 (1906), pp. 90–104, 146–61.

Bricqueville, E. de. *Les Ventes d'instruments de musique au XVIIIᵉ siècle*. Paris 1908.

Burney, C. *The Present State of Music in France and Italy*. London 1771; ed. P. Scholes, London 1959.

The Present State of Music in Germany, the Netherlands and United Provinces. London 1773; ed. P. Scholes, London 1959.

Carreno, T. *Possibilities of Tone Color by Artistic Use of the Pedals*. Cincinnati 1919.

Chaulieu, C. 'Des pédales du piano'. *Le Pianiste* 9 (Paris 1833–4), pp. 131–2.

Ching, J. *Points on Pedalling*. London 1930.

Clementi, M. *Introduction to the Art of Playing on the Pianoforte*. London 1801, R/1974 with an introduction by S. Rosenblum.

Appendix to the Fifth Edition of Clementi's Introduction. London 1811.

Closson, E. *Histoire du piano*. Brussels 1944; Eng. trans., London 1947, 2/1974.

'Pascal Taskin'. *Sammelbände der Internationalen Musikgesellschaft* (1910–11), pp. 234–67.

Cole, W. 'Americus Backers: Original Forte Piano Maker'. *The Harpsichord and Pianoforte Magazine* 4 (1987), pp. 79–85.

Cramer, J. B. *Instructions for the Pianoforte*. London 1812, 3/1818.

Craw, H. 'A Biography and Thematic Catalog of the Works of J. L. Dussek'. Ph.D. Dissertation, University of Southern California, 1964.

Czerny, C. *Vollständige theoretisch-practische Pianoforteschule*, op. 500. Vienna 1838–9; Eng. trans. London 1938–9.

Supplement (oder vierter Theil) zur grossen Pianoforte Schule. Vienna 1846–6; Eng. trans. London 1846–7.

Deutsch, O. E. *Mozart: A Documentary Biography*. Eng. trans. London 1966.

Eigeldinger, J.-J. *Chopin vu par ses élèves*. Neuchâtel 1970. Eng. trans. as *Chopin, Pianist and Teacher*. Cambridge 3/1986.

Engel, K. *The Pianist's Handbook*. London 1853.

Erard. *Du clavecin méchanique au piano en forme de clavecin*. Catalogue of an exhibition at the Conservatoire National Supérieur de Musique, Paris, June–November 1979.

Farjeon, H. *The Art of Piano Pedalling* op. 55. London 1923.

Fay, A. *Music-Study in Germany*. Chicago 1880.

Fétis, F.-J. 'Improvements in the Construction of Pianos'. *Harmonicon* 5 (1827), pp. 158–9.

Fétis, F.-J. and I. Moscheles. *Méthode des méthodes de piano*. Paris 1837; Eng. trans. London 1841.

Framery, N. E. and P. L. Ginguené. *Encyclopédie méthodique: musique*. Paris 1791–1818.

Gallay, J. *Un inventaire sous la Terreur. Etat des instruments de musique relevés chez les émigrés et comdamnés par H. Bruni*. Paris 1890.

Gerig, R. *Famous Pianists and their Techniques*. Newton Abbot 1976.

Grove, G. ed. *A Dictionary of Music and Musicians*. London 1879–89.

Hallé, C. E. and M. eds. *Life and Letters of Sir Charles Hallé*. London 1896.

Hanks, S. 'Pantaleon's Pantalon: an Eighteenth-Century Musical Fashion' *MQ* 55 (1969), pp. 215–27.

Harding, R. *The Piano-Forte*. Old Woking 2/1978.

Herz, H. *Méthode complète de piano*. Mainz 1838; Eng. trans. London 1839.

Hiller, J. A. *Wöchentliche Nachrichten und Anmerkungen die Musik betreffend*. Leipzig 1766–69.

Hipkins, A. J. *A Description and History of the Pianoforte*. London 1896.

Hipkins, E. *How Chopin Played*. London 1937.

Hubbard, F. *Three Centuries of Harpsichord Making*. Cambridge, Mass. 1965.

Hull, A. E. 'Pianoforte Pedalling'. *Monthly Musical Record* 43 (1913), pp. 31–3,

Hummel, J. N. *Ausführliche, theoretisch-practische Anweisung zum Pianoforte-Spiele*. Vienna 1828; Eng. trans. London 1828.

Johnstone, J. A. *How to Use the Pedal in Piano Playing*. London, n.d.

Jousse, J. *The Pianoforte Made Easy*. London 5/c.1820.

Kalkbrenner, F. *Méthode pour apprendre le pianoforte*. Paris 1830; Eng. trans. London 1862.

Kleczynski J. *The Works of Frederic Chopin and their Proper Interpretation*. Eng. trans. London 1882.

Kloppenburg, W.C.M. *De. Pedalen van de Piano*. Amsterdam 1952.

Köhler, L. *Der Klavier-Pedalzug, seine Natur und künstlerische Anwendung*. Berlin 1882.

Kramer, R. 'On the Dating of Two Aspects in Beethoven's Notation for Piano' in *Beethoven-Kolloquium 1977*. Kassel and Basel 1978, pp. 160–73.

Kreutzer, L. *Das normale Klavierpedal*. Leipzig 1928.

Kuhe, W. *My Musical Recollections*. London 1896.

Kullak, A. *Die Aesthetik des Klavierspiels*. Berlin 1861; Eng. trans. of 3rd edn 1893.

Landon, H. C. R. *Haydn: Chronicle and Works*. London 1976–80.

Latour, T. *Sequel to Latour's Instructions for the Pianoforte*. London 1828.

Lavignac, A. *L'Ecole de la pédale*. Paris 1889.

Lenz, W. von. *Die grossen Pianoforte-Virtuosen unserer Zeit*. Berlin 1872; Eng. trans. New York 1899.

Lindo, A. *Pedalling in Pianoforte Music*. London 1922.

Litzmann, B. *Clara Schumann*. Leipzig 1902–8; Eng. trans. London 1913.

Loesser, A. *Men, Women and Pianos*. New York 1954.

Marmontel, A. *Histoire du piano et de ses origines*. Paris 1885.

　Les Pianistes célèbres. Paris 1878.

Mason, W. *Memoirs of a Musical Life*. New York 1901.

Mathews, W. S. B. *School of the Piano Pedal*. Boston 1906.

Matthay, T. *Musical Interpretation*. Boston 1913.

Mattheson, J. *Critica Musica*. 2 vols., Hamburg 1725.

Maunder, R. 'Mozart's Keyboard Instruments'. *EM* 20 (1922), pp. 107–110.

'The Earliest English Square Piano'. *GSJ* 43 (1989), pp. 77–84.

Méreaux, A. *Les Clavecinistes de 1637 à 1790*. Paris 1867.

Milchmeyer, J. P. *Die wahre Art das Pianoforte zu spielen*. Dresden 1797.

Mobbs, K. 'Stops and Other Special Effects on the Early Piano'. *EM* 12 (1984), ppp. 471–6.

Monro, J. *A New and Complete Introduction to the Art of Playing on the Pianoforte*. London 1820.

Montanari, G. 'Bartolomeo Cristofori'. *EM* 19 (1991), pp. 85–96.

Montgeroult, Madame la Comtesse de. *Cours complet pour l'enseignement du fortepiano*. Paris c.1820.

Moscheles, C. *Aus Moscheles' Leben*. Leipzig 1872; Eng trans. London 1873.

Moscheles, I. *Studies for the Pianoforte* op. 70. London 1827.

Newman, W. *Beethoven On Beethoven: Playing His Piano Music His Way*. New York and London 1988.

'Beethoven's Pianos Versus His Piano Ideals'. *JAMS* 23 (1970), pp. 484–504.

Nicholls, F. C. *The Technique of the Piano Pedals*. Liverpool 1902.

Niecks, F. *Frederick Chopin as a Man and Musician*. London 1888.

'On the Use and Abuse of the Pedal'. *MMR* 6 (1876), p. 179.

Petri, J. S. *Anleitung zur practischen Musik*. Lauben 1767.

Pierre, C. *Histoire du Concert Spirituel 1725–1790*. Paris 1975.

Plantinga, L. *Clementi: His Life and Music*. London 1977.

Pollens, S. 'An Upright Pianoforte by Domenico del Mela'. *GSJ* 45 (1992), pp. 22–8.

'Gottfried Silbermann's Pianos'. *Organ Yearbook* 17 (1986), pp. 103–21.

'The Early Portuguese Piano'. *EM* 13 (1985), pp. 18–27.

'The Pianos of Bartolomeo Cristofori'. *JAMS* 10 (1984), pp. 32–68.

'Three Pianos Signed by Cristofori's Assistant, Giovanni Ferrini'. *GSJ* 44 (1991), pp. 77–93.

Quidant, A. *L'Ame du piano*. Paris 1875.

Reichardt, J. F. *Briefe eines aufmerksamen Reisenden die Musik betreffend*. 2 vols., Frankfurt and Leipzig 1774–6.

Riefling, R. *Piano Pedalling*. London 1962.

Rieger, J. H. *Méthode analytique pour l'étude de pianoforte*. Paris 1820.

Rimbault, E. *The Pianoforte*. London 1924.

Ripin, E. 'Expressive Devices Applied to the Eighteenth-Century Harpsichord'. *Organ Yearbook* 1 (1970), pp. 64–80.

Rowland, D. 'Beethoven's Pianoforte Pedalling' in *Performing Beethoven's Instrumental Music*, ed. Robin Stowell. Cambridge, forthcoming.

'Early Pianoforte Pedalling'. *EM* 13 (1985), pp. 5–17.

'The Nocturne: Development of a New Style' in J. Samson ed., *The Cambridge Companion to Chopin*. Cambridge 1992, pp. 32–49.

Rubinstein, A. *Leitfallen zum richtigen Gebrauch des Pianoforte-Pedals*. Leipzig 1896; Eng. trans. 1897.

Russell, R. *The Harpsichord and Clavichord*. London 2/1973.

Schmitt, H. *Das Pedal des Clavieres*. Vienna 1875; Eng. trans. Philadelphia 1893.

Schnabel, K. U. *Modern Technique of the Pedal*. New York c.1954.

Schonberg, H. *The Great Pianists*. London 1963.

Starke, F. *Wiener Pianoforteschule*. Vienna 1819–20.

Steibelt, D. *Méthode de piano*. Paris and Leipzig 1809.

Streicher, N. *Kurze Bemerkungen über das Spielen, Stimmen und Erhalten der Fortepiano*. Vienna 1801, Eng. trans. Ann Arbor 1983.

Tagliavini, L. 'Giovanni Ferrini and his Harpsichord "a penne e a martelletti"'. *EM* 19 (1991), pp. 399–408.

Thalberg, S. *L'Art du chant appliqué au piano*. Paris 1853.

Türk, D. *Klavierschule, oder Answeisung zum Klavierspielen für Lehrer und Lernende, mit kirtischen Anmerkungen*. Leipzig and Halle 1789, 2/1800, 3/1816.

Venino, A. *A Pedal Method of the Piano*. New York 1893.

Virgil, A. M. *The Piano Pedals*. New York 1912.

Wieck, F. *Clavier und Gesang*. Leipzig 1853; Eng. trans. Boston 1872.

Wolff, C. 'New Research on Bach's *Musical Offering*'. *MQ* 57 (1971), pp. 379–408.

Wythe, D. 'The Pianos of Conrad Graf'. *EM* 12 (1984), pp. 447–60.

Zachariae, E. *Das Kunstpedal an Klavier-Instrumenten*. Vienna 1874.

Zimmerman, P. J. G. *Méthode de piano*. Mainz 1840.

Index